You.next()

MOVE YOUR SOFTWARE DEVELOPMENT CAREER TO THE LEADERSHIP TRACK

Dilbert is a registered trademark of Scott Adams, Inc.

Microsoft and Microsoft Project are either registered trademarks or trademarks of Microsoft Corporation in the United States and/or other countries.

ISBN: 1-4392-0559-0

ISBN-13: 9781439205594

Visit www.YouDotNext.com to order additional copies.

Illustrations by Sarah Sobole

TO OUR MANY TEACHERS

CONTENTS

ACKNOWLEDGMENTS

Both authors have learned uncountable lessons about management, for better or for worse, from mistakes made on the job. Theory and training can provide a logical foundation for any role but a manager's abilities are not truly tested until the consequences of his or her real-world decisions can be evaluated. We have each approached every management action with the right intentions, and we have engaged in deep introspection when things went wrong.

Unfortunately the unwitting teachers in each of those lessons were people who were often adversely affected in the process. Bold actions always seem appropriate while you are planning them, but they often go awry when the complexity of people, products, and companies interplay in real life. We owe a great deal to every person who suffered so that each of us could learn. Those people are our many teachers.

Acknowledgements by Mike Finley

Roger DeLacey was a fantastic first manager. He balanced the needs of people with those of the company and taught me that a manager's care can be an intense comfort for every person on the team.

Lee Smith is unquestionably the person who drew my career out of a technology death spiral and introduced me to increasing responsibility. He taught me that respecting people does not mean being a weak manager. Quite the opposite, personal respect is the best backdrop for many of the toughest management actions.

Of the people I have led, Daniel Bassett and Daniel Gore stand out for their help making me understand how to be a better manager. Working with these guys never felt like management; instead, it was more like cooperation toward greater common goals. Linnea Geiss is a person who can recognize an emerging manager very early and I tapped into that instinct to improve this book.

Mark Schoen directed me through the process of becoming more external and financial in my management approach. I can't say that I perfected these abilities but I learned a great deal in the process and I know there is always more to be learned. Gary Landers is a fantastic financial manager who sharpened my ability to fit technical details into the broader business at the right level of priority.

I learned a lot working on Andy Heyman's leadership team. Before that, I'm not sure I fully recognized the value of every individual in a business. Andy also taught me a lot about the power of clear and concise communication, and he tolerated many of my mistakes as I learned.

Jimmy Fortuna's leadership by influence is something that I have admired and often tried to emulate. Jimmy's ability to achieve through others on a grand scale is an enviable trait for any manager.

Erez and Alon Goren have been my mentors and leaders during most of my career. The objective, apolitical environment that they foster in their companies is the spice that creates equal opportunity for anyone who is willing and competent to do a great job.

I have worked closely with Mike Dudgeon for many years; we learned management together and he often blew me away with ingenious instincts from which I could learn.

Acknowledgements by Honza Fedák

First and foremost, I want to thank Mike for inviting me to cooperate on this book. I do not know anyone who would epitomize better the successful transition from a developer and individual contributor to a confident manager, inspirational leader, and respected coach. His example has been motivating me ever since I met him and it has been a great honor to be able to work on this book with him. We cannot all be like Mike, but we sure can try to come closer!

I also need to thank all my colleagues, past and present. I learned something from every one of them. Some have astounded me by their superior and unique qualities and personalities. Some have awed me with their uncanny ability to work with people. Many openly challenged me whenever I did something silly and gave me a chance to learn from my mistakes. Management is a never ending struggle to maintain what has already been accomplished and to try to make things a little better every day. My colleagues continue to teach me valuable lessons as I constantly reinvent what it takes to do the job well.

Last but not least, I want to thank my loving and understanding wife Marta who gives me unwavering support as I try to find the right balance between professional and personal life. A great manager herself, she makes finding that balance look way too easy!

INTRODUCTION

You.next() is addressed to software development professionals who are seeking career growth. More specifically, it examines the highly misunderstood "management track" option and explains many of the incongruities about leadership that frequently cause new managers to stumble. By helping software developers understand management, their own personal aptitude for it, and how to progress toward a career in it, we hope to provide greater job satisfaction for all readers—whether they ultimately choose a management career, or not. For those who decide to move forward, we have included a solid "how to" foundation that will help with early leadership roles.

Now at different companies, the authors were formerly coworkers who met in 2002. We wrote this book because we believe it has a chance to make a real difference in the lives of people who, like us, are dedicating their careers to the creation of software. We each entered the industry as software developers and we each lived through the transition from individual contributor roles into leadership. Since that time we have watched many others go through the process, often helping them when we could.

Looking back at those experiences, it is clear that we did not know what to expect during the early days of our management careers. We were not alone in that predicament; many new leaders in our relatively new industry find themselves in a management job without any formal training or sufficient guidance. Others who seek management roles don't know how to get started. All of them, like us, have only their own mistakes from which to learn as they stumble through the early months and years. Equipped with the experience and knowledge that we've captured in this book, many careers could be smoother and more successful.

Our personal experience has taught us that the infamously introverted reputation of the stereotypical software developer, while certainly not universally true, is founded in fact. It is no surprise that the subjective, interpersonal, external roles of a leader are fraught with mistakes and difficulty for many of us. As a result, developers are often managed by nontechnical leaders whose actions lead to frustration for everyone. But experience has also shown us that technical abilities are a great foundation for the many objective, fair and precise jobs of a leader. *You.next()* intends to help developers understand the ways in which technical abilities can become leadership assets. In the process, the book will also explain which nontechnical abilities are essential for any role, how to develop them, and why.

Consider the traditionally leadership-oriented traits of charisma and communication. These are largely irrelevant to individual proficiency in software development in the early stages of a career. The obvious result is that our line of work does not tend to create its own "natural" leadership ranks; most developers have to consciously decide to build a new and different skill set if they are to emerge as leaders. But once learned, these skills can improve interactions of all sorts, whether technical, personal or in their intended professional leadership setting.

These are important messages for the changing global community of software developers. Established economies have built an unquenchable thirst for software, and entire nations have responded with a software development service industry. *You.next()* helps software professionals on both sides of this economic phenomenon. Those in developed markets who are facing "outsourcing" pressures will learn how to build timeless skills that are of higher value than their established ability to write software. Their counterparts in developing economies will benefit by adapting more smoothly to the growing demands of their relatively new industry. In both places, software developers can gravitate out of pure technical roles and provide leadership to their companies. These leadership roles are core competencies for businesses in any economy.

As a final point, new technologies constantly challenge the expertise of those who are working in the software development trade. It's an accepted fact that we either stay current with an evolving stream of skills or face becoming obsolete. *You.next()* connects the path to leadership with the idea of new career growth and stability, providing an outlet for some to escape this treadmill. We hope to help developers move into management when that is the right choice. We also want to help some readers avoid management altogether, without the fear of opportunity lost. Most of all, we mean to help every reader achieve a perspective of satisfaction and pride for the work they do—whatever that may be.

Chapter 1

PERSPECTIVES

WHO SHOULD READ THIS BOOK

- Software professionals considering a management career

- Software professionals who are thinking about starting a company

- Software professionals facing outsourcing or other career pressures

- Professionals from outside the software development field who are managing software developers

- Software professionals engaging in long-term career planning

- Anyone who has tried managing software developers but feels they failed or need improvement

MIKE'S PERSPECTIVE

I was nine years old when I read *The Electronic Cottage*, which described a fascinating new world that combined business and math, art and engineering. It was a harbinger of a fantastic new industry that was only just getting started thirty years ago. Ever since then, I've spent about half of my life getting educated and the other half being part of the cottage-cum-empire that is the US software industry today. If you are anything like me, you are somewhere along the path that I followed and you are facing many of the same challenges.

This book is about a very specific one of those challenges: the emergence of the manager within, of the leader who can dazzle and amaze with organizational prowess the same way he or she once did with wizard-worthy software. It is a transformation that some will make easily; if that is you, this book will take out most of the uncertainty of knowing when and how to pull it off. It is also a transformation that others will never choose to make—if that is you, I hope you can find peace with yourself for leaving the management path behind and being very, very good at whatever you do.

My perspective in this book is principally aimed at highly technical people in any "individual contributor" function within a software development organization. The fundamental premise is that abilities that create success in technical roles are often overlooked for management functions, much to the detriment of both the person and the company he or she represents. Famously non-communicative technologists mature into frustrated role players when, in fact, they could have been a reliable and happy source of management talent. Why don't they? Because despite their technical training and prowess, they are missing some important foundation elements:

- They do not understand the fundamentals of effective, polished, interpersonal communication

- They do not understand the simple premises underlying otherwise apparently illogical business decisions

- They do not understand how to evaluate and take career improvement risks

My early career was very fortuitous. I did not know it at the time, but right out of college I had a fantastic manager, then a terrible manager, and finally I worked for a start-up where I had no manager at all. I contrasted these three experiences the way you would compare flavors of ice cream—they were not deep comparisons but more matter-of-fact, as in great habits that I wanted to copy or mental notes about how to avoid making people feel the way bad management experiences sometimes made me feel. All these years later, the reason that this book exists is to bridge a fundamental gap in the software development psyche that has been consistent in many software professionals that I have met since then.

MIKE'S MANAGEMENT USE CASE

We've included these Management Use Cases throughout the book where relevant experiences can help shed some light on the points discussed. You'll see them set off from the main text. These are all true stories, for better or worse. Consider how you would deal with them if they happened to you!

In one of my earliest jobs after college, I became friends with a nice guy who had worked at the company for many years before I arrived. His story shocked me. He explained that he was the sole remaining maintenance programmer for a code base of four hundred thousand lines of COBOL. He knew that code inside and out, and it was all he had ever done.

Married, kids, divorced, retired, and rehired, the code remained with him throughout. He had seen astronauts land on the moon when he was already a professional programmer. Not much was going to impress him, and he was successful (satisfied with himself). I understood how he got where he was, and I respected him—but I was determined not to be that guy myself. I crave challenge, change, opportunity, and influence. Of course, I know he had a great deal of confidence and self-esteem, but I did not want that future for myself.

To put it simply, we are trained to solve problems and to work in teams. We are trained to think about logical conclusions and simulate machines in our heads—even literally dreaming a bug fix sometimes. But few aspects of the formative process for software professionals focus on helping us understand how to be the boss, how to take charge and solve problems that are bigger and more ambiguous than we can handle alone, how to inspire others to perform their best for us, and how to assemble the best teams for all of these results.

I've seen it over and over: the very best developers of software are allowed to implode while a host of other nontechnical leaders are empowered to "handle" these preciously skilled human assets. Under the near-sighted perspective of the short term, software engineers feel pressure to perform their trade faster and better, while managers with no competency in software creation set goals by tossing darts at an imaginary board.

HONZA'S PERSPECTIVE

My early experience in Europe was with a small company started by a couple of technology enthusiasts with a dream. The company was well managed financially, but it was almost a "no management" environment as far as people and projects were concerned. Everyone had responsibility for their own work with very little direction or mentoring. We were expected to learn on our own. It was an excellent place to obtain in-depth technical knowledge, self-sufficiency, and self-motivation. Even though I got a chance to lead other developers, it did not teach me much about practical project and people management.

Then I joined a results-oriented American company that was just establishing their European office. The transition was not too difficult because, in some ways, it was a similar environment to that of the start-up: rapidly growing and developing, with a flat hierarchy, where results were of highest importance. But, it was also different in some ways; a multimillion dollar global business with hundreds of employees offered very different opportunities, and challenges.

Since my very first day on the job, I have been working on challenging projects, cooperating with bright, inspiring people, and serving clients from diverse locations and cultures. But I felt left out of the decision making process early on. Even though I did not want to give up my technical career, I wanted to be able to influence the future of the company more than any individual developer can. I knew that gradually taking on more and more management responsibility was the way to achieve it.

My primary motivation was simple: I wanted to be in charge, more in control of my future and that of my company. I felt like a passenger who is nervous because someone else is driving. If you feel like I did back then and aspire to influence the direction of the company that you work for, you should consider taking on at least some aspects of the management role. After all, it is undeniable that companies are run by managers, and very few board seats are reserved for the best technologists. This book is here to help you on that rocky road, but at the same time, to give you a faithful picture of what it means to manage software development and what the transition entails.

You may already have a fairly good idea of that if you have held a team lead role in the past. If so, you probably know that the reality of it is very different from what you anticipated. After reading this book, you may find out that you would prefer to stay on the technical track, confident in your current direction. If you do that, we want you to feel great about your well founded decision and we wish you luck on your path to technical excellence without regrets about the management career you might have had.

Still, consider this. Even though management is very different than software development, the fundamental problem statement of management, if there is such a thing, appeals to a problem solver's mind. It is an optimization problem in concurrent parameters:

- Time (schedule)

- Cost (people, equipment, space, supplies, telecommunication)

- Quality (defects, requirements)

- Risk (design choices, hiring decisions)

- Strategy (technical direction, market direction)

- Business leverage (invest for the long haul or get paid along the way)

One difference, compared to software development, is that because each of these parameters includes other humans, there is typically much more complexity and unpredictability behind every one of them than you will ever encounter in a typical software system. Solving such a problem is partially an intellectual feat and partially following your best instincts.

Developers who naturally aspire to leadership and want to solve problems of this kind are already ahead of others in management *potential*. But getting onto the management path can be difficult and slow. Other developers are perfectly happy with their technical positions and would never choose the challenge of the management problem over the excitement and creativity of an engineering job. They find a creative outlet in the application of technology without the hindrance of management tasks like personnel reviews, financial reporting, planning, and budgeting.

The great news is that our profession provides individualized careers for all tastes. Rewarding futures await the best technologists and the best managers, complementing each other every step of the way. *You. next()* can help each of these roles understand the other. More importantly, this book will provide you with better insight into the management job so that you can effectively choose the role that is best for you.

As you gain work experience, it is inevitable that you will be considered for leadership over a team or project. You may reject it and choose to fully focus on the technical problems at hand. If you are like most developers, you will be occasionally frustrated with some decisions that are made by others about the team or the project that you are on. If you refuse to lead, you will have to live with the fact that you chose the predictable haven of technology over the responsibility of decision making. Or, one day, your frustration may finally boil over and become ambition: a drive to make things better; to set right the decisions that other managers always seem to get wrong. Good luck! The manager within you is emerging!

"Character dreams courtesy of R.E.M."

Chapter 2

WHY YOU SHOULD THINK ABOUT A CAREER IN SOFTWARE DEVELOPMENT LEADERSHIP

WHAT'S THE MYSTERY?

Management *theory* seems easy: Just tell people what to do! But clearly something is hard about it because managers run big companies and reap big rewards—things that not just anyone can accomplish. That apparent ambiguity and a thousand other questions make it natural for successful technologists to consider remaining in the comfort zone of their expertise rather than risking a "plunge" into management:

- Where does a management career go?

- Will my technical skills be lost over time?

- Will my technical accomplishments be forgotten?

- Do I have the fundamental aptitude for management like I do for technology?

- Aren't there enough managers? How will I differentiate myself if I make a change over to management?

- Will I enjoy what I do? Will my career progress? Or will I just be stuck with no options and end up "back" in development?

- Can I be a successful manager without losing my personal life? Or do I have to become one of the workaholics who boast about the weirdest place (or position) from which they answered e-mail?

Many negative outcomes seem possible, but still the nagging thought keeps creeping in: What if you turn out to be a great leader? Could you make a real difference for lots of software developers every day? And would there be big rewards for you?

MOTIVATION AND COMPENSATION: KEEP IT REAL

Changing career tracks is a serious step. You should consider your prospects and the many possible outcomes before you decide to take that step. Few things are more important to this decision than motivation – specifically, what motivates you and what will continue to motivate you during the long days and longer projects of the coming years. Ten or fifteen years, in fact, would be a reasonable time scale to contemplate.

That is not a simple question. Job satisfaction comes from a number of factors, and to make the situation even more complicated, the factors change over time for all of us. It will be difficult for you to understand whether a management job will keep you interested because you don't yet know what the job really entails. Reading this book will give you some insight into that. You may also want to talk to your manager or a trusted mentor to get their perspective. Ultimately, however, the answer is uniquely your own.

As you think about what motivates you, it is normal and healthy to have compensation high on the list of things which define what you want from your job. There could be a problem, though, if you only want the management job because of a bigger paycheck. You may get short-term results but fail in the long term when the job is radically different from what you enjoy doing. If that happens, you will have a hard time motivating yourself to be passionate and intense as a leader. You can't fake it; without passion, you will fail to improve yourself over time and you will not excel in your management career.

On the other hand, a healthy ambition for cash compensation can provide intense fuel for your trip down the management track. There's no doubt that companies reward people who are willing to take responsibility by giving them a portion of the benefits of their success. Management can be a great path to get more cash—a lot more for the best managers. But the devil is in the details: Many good technologists earn big pay packages too, and a spike in market demand for developers can quickly increase developers' salaries above those of their direct managers.

To make things worse, management roles generally have their compensation leveraged—that is, tied to the success of the business—which means that the risk of failure is, in some part, passed along to the management team. They earn less money when the business is less successful and more if financial goals are met by the company. Very few developers would ever accept that sort of risk without a much larger reward, such as occurs in software start-up companies. You should look at increasing your compensation as a goal for your management career only if you are confident in your ability to drive success and to become a manager for the long haul.

It may seem awkward that we would discuss your confidence about long-term roles in leadership when you are only now considering seriously how to *start* leading. But the fact is that you are making a big decision and it will be difficult to reverse so you owe it to yourself to contrast the career paths as much as you can.

LONG TERM CONSIDERATIONS FOR SOFTWARE DEVELOPMENT ROLES

Every career is different and clearly there will always be many people who have long-term success without ever stepping into a leadership role. But some of those people have ideas or thoughts about leadership and simply don't act on them. On any given day, other things are more important; over the long-haul, nothing happens. The drive to lead lacks urgency in the face of constant programming pressures. Like many looming disasters, we fail to see the threat until it is too late.

MIKE'S MANAGEMENT USE CASE

My first job out of college was full of excitement and promise. The other new grads and I were going to set the world on fire with our sheer will to make brilliant technology. We had all been highly recruited, and we felt select and valued. But it turned out to be a disaster.

The work was not challenging, and the schedules were too slow. The recruiters were the most inspiring people at the company, so once we were on board, the vision seemed to be lost. Endless "process training" was followed by endless process repetition. Most of us were planning to leave or find our way onto one or two interesting teams.

We learned enough about the products to realize that they were inadequate, but the process would not allow us to do what was needed to set them right. The word "quality" was used as an excuse for every inefficient, dumb, and boring part of the job. It was no surprise that the company announced layoffs within a few months.

I have a vivid memory of watching a tractor-trailer loaded with sod pulling up to our facility with an army of groundskeepers as the overhead speaker called out the names of my colleagues who were now jobless. Of course, the situation was complex, and the company reached it one well-intentioned step at a time. But clearly, both management and development teams were impossibly off-course.

THREAT ONE: THE PACE OF TECHNOLOGY CHANGE

Change is inevitable. The fact is that there is no safety in retaining a perpetual role as an individual contributor in software development. Technology moves very fast—it can be overwhelming. You may be comfortable and even proud of keeping pace now but you have to think about the future and what it may bring. There is no such thing as *status quo* in software development because the craft itself is perpetually in flux.

Management, on the other hand, is challenging in a completely different way; it is based on economics, which will not change as fast, and psychology, which is nearly timeless. From this perspective, a move into a management role can be empowering in the short term and also a more stable base from which to build your future.

Think about it this way. As a software developer, you can progress in technical skill, work ethic, and product knowledge until you are intensely valuable to your company and customers. But there is nearly always a limit to what you will be paid. A manager—of software development or any function—is bound only by her or his ability to scale and take on ever-larger organizations. In other words, even assuming that software compensation will continue to increase and that you will stay current and build a better and better skill set, a management career *may* have even more to offer. Beware! You also *may* be a much better developer than you ever will be a manager—you'll never know unless you try.

THREAT TWO: GLOBALIZATION

Software development outsourcing is another factor in the career of every technology professional, whether you are above or below the global average wages for the work you do. Outsourcing is a big change and brings with it the angst and stresses associated with tectonic shifts in our field. If you are in an economy that is losing software development jobs to a lower-priced market, the odds are high that your company is soon going to be forced to consider focusing on core competencies in functional areas other than software development. That does not mean that great software developers won't be needed any longer, just that software development as a core competency will no longer be center stage. Instead, competency in product design, marketing, customer service or sales become preeminent. Those roles become the new target for the best careers in the company, and fortunately, every one of those functions will make use of your new management capabilities.

If, on the other hand, you are in an economy that is receiving software development jobs, you are likely to be part of a company that specializes in software development *practices* as a core competency, not in the features and specifics of the product that is being developed. So the pressure on you is to grow in your ability to formalize and implement software processes with newer and more powerful tools, delivering quality as a way of concretely measuring effectiveness. In these service-oriented organizations, *people are the product,* so management and product development become synonymous.

THREAT THREE: SOFTWARE HEROES

Many software developers who build a deep skill set in a specific functional area, along with a productive and profitable code base, simply become too valuable to be promoted into management roles. These developers are the heroes of a start-up or even of an established company. The very fact of the success of the code creates a crushing workload that stops the hero from pursuing training or receiving meaningful career coaching. The cash and the cachet of the role keep him or her motivated to continue the heroics.

The entire business or product line may be constrained by what the hero can achieve, until that is no longer sufficient and the team must grow. The hero could become the manager, but usually he or she must ensure the integrity of the product while someone else focuses on the new people. And so, after years of technical toil, obsolescence catches up and the hero is just one more developer, wondering where the cachet and career went. Rewarded with stock options or money, depending on the resources of the company, these engineers are trapped by their own excellence.

THREAT FOUR: YOUR EGO

You may like to consider yourself "more" than an engineer—something closer to an artist of the electronic milieu. If so, you may feel that a move into management would waste your genius and jeopardize the expression of your craft, even though other frustrations or goals have made you consider it.

That is a natural feeling—great software developers are artists in the vein of the architect. "Clean" source code in any language carries an aesthetic that is evident to any master of the form, and high-level design is typically called architecture in software development for good reason. The thrill of seeing your design in action is a potent drug that can be hard to give up on your way to management. The *inner beauty of software* is immediately visible to its creator.

While romantic, this view of the Java Hemingway is not a reliable future for most people. A growing trend in software engineering is to assemble existing components, proven design patterns and third party subsystems into functional high-quality and predictable tools. Developers of these systems are skilled, practical and capable engineers rather than free spirited artists. New terminology and nomenclature describe their work tools, which bear evidence of the transition from art to trade. The result is more about scale and quality than about genius and imagination.

As the whole of software development matures, more and more of it is becoming a commodity: you can purchase databases, messaging systems, UI components, Web publishing frameworks, and whole working systems that need only to be customized. The value of aesthetics in software development is undeniable, but a fact of growth in our field is that practicality of function often outweighs the subtle benefits of form.

This is not the same as saying that all developers are equal. Of course the whole field is widely differentiated and the best developers are several dozen times more productive, and more highly rewarded than the rest. The simple point is that very few developers, if any, will remain employed merely for the aesthetic value of their work product.

MIKE'S MANAGEMENT USE CASE

Money and power are not good reasons to enter management. If you go into it for the title and bonus plan, you will most likely overlook many of the things that you need to learn.

Case in point was a developer who came to me time and time again asking for more work and more money. At first, he succeeded, becoming a fantastic developer and earning several raises, but then he reached a point where I could not pay him more. He began insisting on a team leadership role because the company was growing and there seemed to be a fast-track career path in management.

He got the role but acted far too aggressively, angering everyone on his team and ultimately failing to deliver a release. Years later, he is back on track as a very successful independent contractor. He never tried management again.

SURPRISE: YOU ARE ALREADY QUALIFIED TO LEAD

It is a daunting prospect. On one hand, you can keep your current job with known upside (problem-solving, learning new tools, products, and technologies) but with the risk of potential obsolescence and globalization of your role. On the other, you may be attracted to a career in management, but you are paralyzed when you consider your wildly variable chances of success or failure on that path. The choice may seem so difficult, so fundamental that you just can't talk yourself into a decision. But if you don't make up your mind then you are leaving it up to chance, which is worse. Careers in either the technical arena or in leadership are going to challenge you. Choose one and develop that competency.

Management of software engineering is not the natural evolution for every software developer's career. A deep technical track is a more suitable path for some, while others will take to it like ducks to water. It is a question of choice based on your interest and ability— and you may question your ability to the point that you never decide to try it out. But rest assured, you are already qualified. The following table shows analogous elements of what a software developer does and what a manager does. Though it is not immediately evident to someone outside the field, the skills of a software developer are in fact a reasonable mapping of many of the skills that are needed to manage:

Developer Role	Manager Role
Design software	Design processes and organizations
Code	Project planning and execution
Test	Measure progress against goals
Debug	Remove obstacles to projects or teams
Deploy	Run new business programs

Learn new technologies	Learn new business concepts
Perform code reviews	Program or status reviews
Attend developer conferences	Attend trade fairs or shows
Program "for fun" at home	Read about management "for fun" on the beach
Experiment with design tools	Experiment with new methodologies
Tinker	Micromanage
Visit live deployments to troubleshoot	Visit live clients to get shot
Add debugging code to troubleshoot	Bring in experts to drive closure on a release

Despite the similarities in these columns, it is undeniable that the "management track" takes software developers further and further away from technology. The demands of schedules and finances, people and planning, all take more time with each stage of organizational growth. New skills have to be developed and pitfalls are all around in this unfamiliar territory. Even so, when it comes to the challenge of managing software development, anyone who has been a software developer has a fundamental advantage over anyone who has never been in the role before. The advantage shows itself in many different strategic ways—whether it is intuition about how a new technology will disrupt the R&D cycle or understanding why a project is on or off track and how to fix it, or any one of many others.

Most developers do not see any career options in front of them, blind to the richness that is in plain sight. The skills of a developer are valuable in many roles, not just in development or in development management. The beauty of a career that starts in software development is that it places you at the heart of the operation of whatever your company does. Software links computers and people together—measuring, tracking, testing, and checking everything. You can do many things from there, depending on what you choose. Technical sales, accounting, and product management—these are all roles that will leverage deep knowledge of a product, software development process, and customers that you have gained in your technical role. Each of them has a need for growth as the business expands, and there are valuable things you can do while you learn the ropes of a new job function.

MIKE'S MANAGEMENT USE CASE

During a sales slump at my company a few years back, the "water cooler" talk was abuzz with anger and frustration because our products lacked features and quality. I felt that the other developers and I were doing a great job, pouring our hearts and minds into product development, but the low sales results were undeniable. Among many possible conclusions, I guessed that we had a communication problem: the priority of required features was not getting from the "front lines" to the development team. The reverse was probably also true: our request for additional time to deliver higher quality was probably never making it to our clients.

I was right—by pulling a sales person and an account manager into a meeting to hash through some simple examples, I was able to determine that our processes had introduced so many checkpoints and sign-offs that we had become process-bound.

I took this finding to my boss, a trusted and intelligent person, who quickly dismissed my concerns as no more than anecdotes. Furthermore, he said that by talking with sales and account managers, I had created an additional channel of communication that would be sure to damage our ability to maintain standard processes. I spent a miserable twenty-four hours, considering whether I had misjudged my boss and my company, or whether he could actually have been right. Fortunately for me, the very next day, he apologized and together we took immediate steps to solve the core problem. What a relief!

IF NOT YOU, THEN WHO?

A sensible way to build an organization in many disciplines is to promote from within, choosing people who are good individual contributors but also show a natural tendency to lead. The military is probably a good example of a career in which these traits are aligned—great soldiers are passionate and inspiring leaders by their sheer actions and abilities.

Conventional wisdom says that software development, by comparison, is just the opposite. It would appear that the things that make great developers great are precisely the things that stop them from being leaders, and vice versa. Independent work and fussy attention to detail are considered wise for a developer but uninspiring in a team leader. Flowery presentations that explain how a new organization works can excite and align teams but would never pass muster in a technical design review.

This conventional wisdom is flawed on many levels, but the central problem with it is that individual *abilities* are mistakenly identified as individual *limitations*. Software developers practice a truly modern blend of creativity and engineering, inventing nomenclatures to describe problems in a way that people and machines can parse. Their abilities are simply misunderstood because theirs is a relatively new discipline, with few established practices or accepted metrics. There are many great leaders in most software development teams, but the work they undertake every day does not reflect an outsider's concept of leadership.

HONZA'S MANAGEMENT USE CASE

The artificial link between abilities and limitations is often self-imposed. I had a chance to work with a smart developer who nonetheless refused to improve his soft skills such as team work or communication. He argued that a developer had to be talented, intelligent, and knowledgeable but that soft skills were not necessary. He pointed out several examples of well known technologists who were very poor at those skills and inferred that soft skills in fact seem to be the exact opposite of what defines a great developer!

It is true that hard skills are typically more important than soft skills in software development. But it is a mystery to me why so many perfectly logical developers conclude that soft skills therefore do not matter at all or even that improving them will somehow dull or weaken their technical abilities. It is as if the flaws of our role models become engrained as desirable traits to be mimicked.

The limitations of someone that you admire do not define your own boundaries. The developer I was working with insisted on a false image of an ideal role model to the point of lowering his value and potential for the team and for the company.

"Upper" management from outside of the software development area has a difficult time understanding which developers want to be leaders, which ones can be effective leaders, and which ones can be spared from their technical duties to take on management tasks. Taking the most obvious "born" leaders who are available from the development ranks seldom provides enough people to run the whole organization. Other individuals who stand out for their technical contribution are out of reach for management because of their value as direct contributors. This can even lead to the absurd point when less capable people get promoted into leadership just because they are the only available team members who can be easily spared from their current positions. The bottom line is that unless the software organization has experienced strong and prolonged growth, it most likely lacks a culture of promoting enough software developers into leadership roles.

MIKE'S MANAGEMENT USE CASE

A friend and I were paired to work on a project because our software would have to interact in the final deliverable. We were indoctrinated in the process of software development and given a nine-month schedule. We finished in four weeks and were told to wait for the rest of the team.

The plan called for all developers to have identical skills and performance. It also assumed that all parts of the project would require equal expertise. That made planning simple, but completely unrealistic. In reality, no two developers had the same skills and the job estimates were impossibly flawed. During our idle time, we focused on inventing new products at first, then on providing software "demos" for these concept products.

> Both of us left the organization before the "official" project finished. It was a great company with a long past and a bright future. How could they get it so wrong?

In the absence of a clear and self-sustaining leadership structure for software development teams, many companies resort to placing management talent from other disciplines over the software development organization. Sometimes this works, sometimes it fails miserably, but every time it is discouraging to the next generation of software development leaders who are emerging. Some of these potential leaders choose not to make the move into management because they are simply afraid of becoming *like* the people to whom they report. And that fact means there are more management roles for more poor managers to fill, completing a downward cycle.

BREAK THE CYCLE

The state of the industry today demonstrates a lack of technical management talent. Late schedules, projects over budget, quality complaints from consumers, and data security gaps are just a few of the consequences of misaligned teams and leaders.

Be brutally honest with yourself about whether or not management is the right direction for you at this point in your career. If you don't enjoy solving ambiguous problems over a long period of time, the rewards of management will not stimulate you to advance. Technical careers are characterized by mechanistic, deterministic problems, and objective measurements; these are luxuries that a management career will not provide. If you get frustrated or even depressed when people don't behave predictably like *systems* do, your management career will have a difficult start. Many proven personality tests are available online for you to take. They can offer a good deal of insight for a small investment of your time.

If you still want larger responsibilities, and don't know exactly how to get them, then you are what we call an *emerging manager*. Visualize yourself sometime in the future with the abilities that you will have as an established and successful leader. Since you are an individual contributor now, your goal of emerging into a leadership role has to be achieved through an evolution into that future state. Your evolution has two distinct dimensions: your capability to manage and the organization's recognition of that ability. Neither of these has to occur first. The logical progression is to gain the capability and then to be promoted into the role. The opposite, that is promotion before capability, is a different and much less predictable route, but it is sometimes unavoidable, such as the "battlefield promotion" where someone must take charge, so someone does.

Regardless of the order in which capability and promotion occur, they are separate processes, and you should think of them as such. If you work to be recognized and promoted before you are capable, you may get what you wanted but then find yourself dissatisfied and unsuccessful. On the other hand, if you work toward the capabilities of management, you may become frustrated after building competencies that go unrecognized for some time. The best strategy will be to take steps toward building your skills while raising your profile in the organization, emerging as a leader in the eyes of current and future peers.

CLOSURE

You may not know everything about the leadership track, but you do know there is such a thing and you are curious. You keep thinking that you should do something about your career, for the long term, but it seems like a big effort and you are already under a lot of stress. You have always relied on your technical skills so why take a chance on unproven abilities now?

Unless you have decided on a firm direction for your career, this chapter should have provided you with some food for thought and points to consider when addressing that question. Hopefully it helped you realize that you are already better equipped to be on the management track than you previously assumed.

For now, keep thinking about your motivation, ambitions, and passions. Envision what you want your career to look like in five, ten, or fifteen years. Be sure to factor in the impact of changing technology and competition in our industry. What do you have to do if you want to be the most efficient coder in the building? The most admired architect? A functional expert in a specific area? And what if you want to be a successful manager and leader? Read on.

Chapter 3

THE EMERGING MANAGER

Every career has rewards and frustrations—highs and lows that surround inflexion points when major transitions occur. As a software developer, your career is no exception, and you have probably considered many possibilities:

- Your next promotion

- New responsibilities

- A new employer

- New technology

- Additional formal education

Knowing how to advance your career with certainty is nearly impossible. But you *can* get a better sense of how to advance toward each possible inflexion point, and what kind of job satisfaction or success lies beyond that choice. Armed with this information, you may simply become certain that your career is already on the right path, which is a highly valuable comfort zone. Or you might gain conviction about making a career change; either way is an improvement.

IS THIS THE RIGHT TIME?

If you are not asking yourself where to go next in your career, it's probably not time to make a move into management. The question of how long you should remain an individual contributor is a very personal one. It should be long enough, certainly, to have proven yourself on the job—facing real problems like tough bugs deep in the software, difficult client feedback, and the occasional deadbeat teammate. As long as you find the job challenging and you are learning new things at a fast pace, your current role still has potential. But you do not want to stay in that role so long as to become part of the landscape—unable to move on because of the depth of undocumented knowledge that you hold or trapped by an otherwise irrelevant skill set that you have not updated.

You are not ready to move on if what you want is to manage a software team so that you can demote your antagonists or promote your friends. It is not the right approach for someone who is simply trying to find a way to exert technical ideas that have been repeatedly rejected by competent engineers. It is not a means to avoid obsolescence or the "right next step" when personal life changes take place. For the long haul, these motivators are not sufficient to get you over the challenges and initial failures of learning to manage. You need the deeper stamina that comes from a desire to help others succeed. Any shorter-term purpose will end badly for the individual, the company, and the industry as a whole.

Consider the categories in the following columns:

Not Ready For Management	Emerging Manager
Feels like management team is incompetent because they are not emphasizing technology.	Wonders what other skills or knowledge the management team has because their insights and actions do not seem to follow a technical rationale.
Feels like teammates are competitors (the good ones) or incompetent (the bad ones).	Realizes that the point of the team is getting more done, more predictably, than what any one person can do alone. There's enough work for almost everyone, even if some people are noticeably better than others at the job.
Does not feel confident in the value of the work being done—what's the point of the product or even the company? These are logical questions but asking them would reveal that you don't know the answers, so you never ask.	Feeling that you have progressed to a world-class level of development capability—technically as a developer and commercially for creating valuable products. Realization that you have contributed to the team in a meaningful way and you want to make other people have that same feeling.

MIKE'S MANAGEMENT USE CASE

I was at a very productive peak with a generation of technology and tools a few years ago. At that time, my company was highly dependent on a single product that I had helped create, so I felt a great deal of responsibility for client satisfaction. We were growing fast, with tremendous opportunities ahead, and I knew it. It was the kind of promise that attracted veteran executives to come help us.

In the wee hours of one morning, I was still at the office debugging a problem when a new exec saw me and came over. From that conversation, I expected to share some technology and gain some insight—to me, we were colleagues with common goals burning the late-night oil. Instead, he told me I should go home.

I was outraged—worse: demoralized. He did not know my responsibility, and he obviously did not appreciate the work I was doing. Why would he sabotage my pride of workmanship and sap away my self-worth with those words? If I thought I could leave, then of course I would. It took me a long time to understand his words. What he meant was, "Why aren't you managing someone to do this work tomorrow? If it is this important, then something else can be re-prioritized. You are too important for the long term to burn out now." Of course, the answer is simple: I was not yet a manager.

EMERGING MANAGER STEP ONE:
MANAGE YOURSELF

The first action, one you can start working on right now, is to manage yourself well. Set specific goals that you can work hard to meet, and always meet them. Stretch these goals to cover intermediate results like learning new technologies or keeping up with the industry that your company serves instead of just completing your assignments. Avoid petty issues and communicate crisply and proactively about what is happening in your work. If you achieve all of that, you will become a model software engineer long before you are a manager. This advice may help you enjoy your engineering role more and perhaps you will never choose to move toward management.

A second aspect of managing yourself is to try to stay out of the critical path of your current project. This may seem counterintuitive, but in fact it is central to the idea of leadership that you must master. If you are the only one who can perform certain functions, then you are limiting how much of that function can be done at any one time. You are stopping other people from learning that function. You are making everyone dependent on yourself, which is disempowering to everyone else as they go about their jobs. You will be under pressure to deliver results day-to-day, which will stop you from taking steps for improvement in the long term. It is acceptable, and sometimes unavoidable, to be on the critical path for a while but don't make it a habit.

Consider how other people think of your work. Being too possessive of a deliverable or a specific skill may seem like the right way to demonstrate ownership over an area of competence. You may even expect management responsibility to follow naturally because of the productivity that you demonstrate through intense work. But the reality is that once you establish yourself as the cornerstone for a technical area, you cannot be relieved of responsibility for that area without a good deal of time and effort from other people. So you will in fact be denied the opportunity for management *because of the needs of the business*. More than likely, it will be assumed that you would prefer to stay at the individual contributor level and that you would be demoralized if asked to make a move into management.

HONZA'S MANAGEMENT USE CASE

The transition from individual contributor to team lead was a rocky one for me. I understood perfectly that code was a shared resource that had to be maintainable by everyone. In fact, I was doing all the right things to make it work that way: structure it well, document it thoroughly, stick to established coding styles, etc. But after I invested so much into the code, I got personally attached to it. Even though my intention was to make it accessible to other people, I could not bear to see what the other people did when they got their hands on it.

Worse yet, I found it much easier to correct other people's changes to *my* code rather than explain what they should have done differently. I ended up correcting and re-doing a lot of other people's work, wasting my time, discouraging others, and slowing down the team progress.

It took quite a while before I realized that, in order to be effective, I should focus on explaining what I expect rather than fixing it myself. I was stuck, unable to scale into bigger projects, until I accepted a simple truth: the code may be slightly imperfect—or different than what I would have developed personally—but no single person can supervise every last line of code without becoming a project bottleneck.

EMERGING MANAGER STEP TWO:
EXCELLENT DOCUMENTATION

By documenting the business problem that your software solves, or the specifics of what the software has to do (and why), you can remain independent of the code that you create. Yes, it takes more time to document for posterity, but the alternative is that you *are* the posterity of that code until you and the code become irrelevant or obsolete. Hardly a good alternative, whether you choose management or not!

Don't get hung up in the absence of process steps or standard templates for documentation—just make your own and enforce your own policy about when and what to document. Soon enough you'll have a handy document to provide when anyone asks you a question, and not too long after that, the document will be accessed by all without your even knowing it. Don't be surprised if important things about your product or market have never been documented by anyone before you; use whatever is there but don't wait for someone else to start capturing it all on paper. Be fastidious about keeping the documentation updated, too; documentation lives just like programs do.

A side benefit of great documentation is that it facilitates training. If your work becomes important and there is a need to engage other people in it, you will be encouraged to train others. It's the only way your management team can avoid the inherent risk that is associated with having one person with key *business continuity* knowledge. What happens if you win the lottery and move on to a life of hacking 1970s microcontrollers in a Caribbean paradise? If you have documentation ready, you will have an easy time when the training opportunity arises. Through training, you will find that you can easily create a set of willing followers. Technical peers will be impressed when you teach them the things you know—not because of what you taught but because you were chosen to teach, prepared for it, and capable of doing it.

If you are not the best technician, find a dimension of yourself that people on the team admire, even if it is a personal dimension. Use advice in this dimension to establish respect. Parlay respect into willing followers by providing options about important topics of leadership that you can later demonstrate to be true.

EMERGING MANAGER STEP THREE: OUT OF THE BOX

A good deal of an emerging manager's talent and time should be spent understanding the external influences on his or her software development organization. Ask how priorities are set, not just what are the priorities. Ask why specific deadlines are important, not just what has to get done. Don't be shy about asking questions that may seem naïve; it would be far worse to remain ignorant of the answers. You will be surprised at how often you will actually teach something in the process of learning, and at how often your seemingly simple and basic questions uncover potential problems or opportunities for improvement.

By engaging in product definition activities, business purpose discussions, and client affairs, you can suggest alternatives that would not be obvious to someone with a different skill set. In doing so, you become part of the framework that is outside of the traditional software developer's scope; you are out of the box.

Dwelling on external influences is counterintuitive for many software developers. They are in the business because they love to solve puzzles and write programs, or because the money was good compared to other fields, or because they had a knack for breaking other people's software in high school. Someone else always gave them the assignment, handing over the question or specification in neat terms. Having to understand why their own employer wants to create software or why a client wants to buy it may at first seem to be a foreign concept. But a majority of people like to understand their place and role in the world so chances are that you too will like the learning process. Our recommendation is that you at least try to take this step, and then determine for yourself whether if feels like a comfortable, or stressful, part of your daily activities.

The discussions won't be technical, or at least not by your standards, but sound thinking and a logical approach will always be well received. There is no taboo barring such involvement, but no-one will suggest your participation unless you show initiative and interest first. You will have to be bold; for example, ask people in leadership roles all around you if you can help with non-development activities that will broaden your horizons. Cultivate acquaintances you have made outside of product development, injecting any wisdom you can offer into conversations that come up. There is no specific formula but accumulated experience gained in this way will add valuable context to your daily activities building software now, and it will create opportunities for you as a leader later on. Examples:

- Ask if you can help prepare reports and presentations. You'll have to commit to this above and beyond the scope of daily work and within a constrained time line. If you're not ready to do that, you may not be ready to take on more responsibility through leadership.

- Ask if you can attend the department leadership meeting, even if only as a listener. Suggest that you might need to be ready to represent the group when the manager is next on vacation. Don't be discouraged if the answer is no; there may be sensitive subjects in the meeting that you are simply not eligible to hear based on corporate rules.

- Ask how decisions are made about projects and budgets, hiring and features. Find out who makes these decisions. Suggest ways that you can get involved researching or discussing these topics based on knowledge you have built up independently. (And make sure you have something relevant to add!)

- Find out when financial reporting periods happen and be part of the process.

EMERGING MANAGER STEP FOUR:
BECOME A FUNCTIONAL LEADER

You have a key asset working for you: what you do as a developer is *something*. By comparison, the entire activity set of management at every level above you is *nothing*. This may seem odd, but the fact is that the management structure exists to create and foster the activities of the people who actually do *something*. If you take everyone who does not manage anyone else out of the business, the business will stop. On the other hand, without the leadership structure, odds are high that things would not continue going well for very long either. Both structures are different in their purpose, but one cannot exist without the other. Your management decision is, fundamentally, to switch sides between these symbiotic partners.

One way to start is by becoming a *functional leader*. Consider your current organization and the people you work with every day. You can probably identify the functional leaders who are the "go-to" people in some area of the product or process used by your company. These individuals are often admired and successful in long-term roles. The most obvious ones dominate one area and are key contributors to the business, with no clear plan to identify a successor. They are proud of the knowledge and capability they hold, and they are admired by peers and customers for it.

You may be one of these yourself—often emerging managers have gone quite far down the functional leadership path before reaching a high level of frustration for what they feel is a lack of recognition of their ability. The fact of the matter is that what they do is important, but the business does not run on one person's capability. For the business to grow, that person has to grow too. If the functional leader does not scale up, other managers will identify this "ingrown" bottleneck and try to work around it. One way or another, the business *will* grow if it is creating value. The functional leader will either fail, becoming sidelined into a maintenance role, or this same leader will emerge and grow *with* the business by learning to lead *people*.

STEPS TOWARD BECOMING A FUNCTIONAL LEADER

- Pick a neglected area of knowledge that no one seems to know much about but everyone needs to know more about. Often this will be in the form of a poorly documented and complex portion of the product. But beware! Don't get trapped by becoming a subject matter expert to the point that you cannot escape to do bigger things.

44

- Avoid the "librarian syndrome" whereby you merely collect and regurgitate facts, albeit in an expert manner. As a functional leader, you must provide vision and leadership linking information to plans and actions.

- Complete a minor feat within the subject matter to prove your competence and then announce within your peer group that you plan to own this domain for everyone's benefit. If you have credibility on the technology and you keep a great attitude when people start engaging you, soon you will be a "go-to" person when leadership is needed. Collect information feverishly and publish it in coherent documentation very publicly.

- Take immediate ownership over areas related to this information and work diligently to provide organized and coherent information about the status of any efforts that require it.

Like functional leadership, the ability to lead *people* comes easier to some individuals. If you are already a natural at leading people or if you've worked on this capability, you likely have enough of it to emerge as a manager. You do not need intense depth in this area. You are more likely to do it wrong thinking that it is *more* complex than it actually is. If you think you lack leadership skills, the most important thing for you to do is relax about it. Realize that what is required of you is not difficult, but it does take practice.

EMERGING MANAGER STEP FIVE:
CREATE WILLING FOLLOWERS

The idea of *willing followers* is well developed in management literature. It refers to a very basic idea, namely that people must be willing to follow your direction if you are to manage them. As software developers, we are accustomed to being willing followers without even knowing it. That makes the effort of becoming the *leader* somewhat unnatural and daunting. The most chronically technical software developers who seek management roles can sometimes appear to be in denial about the free will of their team members. Watch out! An overbearing and dominant new manager will be rejected quickly by experienced, talented software teams.

MIKE'S MANAGEMENT USE CASE

I went through a hard core-phase as a team lead. I thought I knew everything about everything and that my job was to intimidate people into achievement like a drill sergeant. I cringe at the stunts I pulled, for better and often for worse. I got into the habit, for example, of stopping meetings to call on people who would validate or contradict what anyone else was saying. I reasoned that by forcing different opinions to face off in a dogfight, problems would be solved faster and more effectively.

Of course, this approach alienated great people who needed a nurturing environment, where conflict could be resolved in a more private and productive way. People who knew me then still remind me of something I said when a developer gave me an estimate that I thought was too high for the job: "OK, if that's your final answer, then you and I will each start coding our own versions of it today and whoever finishes first still has a job. Ready?" I did get the developer to lower his estimate with that kind of mindless intimidation, but he left the company within a few weeks. He was talented, and I took that value away from my company. I denied him pride and dignity because I was so shortsighted.

"Willing followers" is a topic worth reading about elsewhere. For the immediate, there are really very few points on which to focus. In order for people to follow you, you need to:

- Be admirable

- Be fair

- Be informed

- Be accessible

- Listen

The good news is that you can do them all.

A. BE ADMIRABLE

Admirable people come in all shapes and sizes. It's not about being someone who people want to *be*—it's about being someone who others believe is going to be *successful*. Don't erase your own individuality trying to conform to the pop-culture version of admiration, but *do* govern yourself according to some key behaviors:

- Dressing and grooming. No excuses here…if you need a makeover, get one. Your career depends on it, and you can act on it immediately. If this point makes you uncomfortable, it probably applies to you. You can be a technical leader with body odor and a ripped T-shirt, but that's not why you are reading this book. Dress appropriately and be clean, always. If you think manners are unimportant, put this book down and get one about etiquette. If you don't know a barber or hair stylist on a first-name basis, solve that problem today.

- Don't break the rules. Be on time, be prepared, and don't break company policy. Don't abuse the system. This is not a commandment to become your worst management stereotype. You can still be uniquely yourself without being an outward rebel. Concentrate on achieving a management role so you can change the rules you don't like.

- Respect everyone, all the time. You don't have to agree with every management decision, but you do have to support the ones that are made by others. You don't have to like everyone, but you cannot set anyone aside or speak of anyone critically unless it is objective and directed to them. Don't disparage anyone or any department—not even a competitor or an ex-employee.

MIKE'S MANAGEMENT USE CASE

A coworker was going through a messy divorce. We were all crashing up against a deadline, but he came to my desk, obviously distressed, and said that he had to leave for a few days. I knew he would be struggling to remain effective if he stayed at work and I also knew that I would be working well into the evening, with or without him. I shook his hand, looked at him in the eye and told him I had him covered—he could go in peace and return when his mind was settled. I could see the weight lift off of him as he went, and I felt the full brunt of that weight when I saw the sun come up from my desk after working all night to finish his work and mine. Years later, he has repaid my loyalty a hundredfold with his own. His unwavering confidence in me fueled my fledgling early move into a leadership role.

B. BE FAIR

The reason that leaders from different organizations can come together and forge a common plan when needed is that they are all fair. True leaders can set differences aside and point the organization in the direction of the best collective outcome for everyone. They don't use their position to advance an agenda that is not in the best interest of the business as a whole. For you, that means that you will include everyone when you share news and listen to everyone when they express an opinion. You will be surprised how many people will become your willing followers when you get their opinion and include it in your perspective. To be sure, you will get some crazy opinions, but the point is that you listen and apply judgment, not ridicule.

C. BE INFORMED

If you build a reputation as someone who is informed, people will gravitate naturally to your leadership. Learn about company policies for benefits, about the company's senior leadership and their experience, about competitors and their product's capabilities, about your product's acceptance in the marketplace and anything else that is interesting. You can get a lot of this information from public places like the Internet—it's amazing how many people grow in their jobs as functional leaders, but never read the company's Web site or press releases. As you research and learn, use this information freely to "connect the dots" for people around you. You may find that you can link events in the company's communications, such as a new member of the board of directors, or a new project that is starting, to a strategic objective that is stated in the annual report. (Another document that is all too often unread!)

Seek out senior managers and ask them to take you to lunch. Often, you can get the people who interviewed you to agree to this simply because they were part of bringing you on board (no matter how long ago that was). Or use a company-wide e-mail announcement that you received as a springboard to start a conversation. You will find that managers "far above" you thirst to know about how *your* team is doing as a proxy for the company as a whole. From them, you want to know the long-term strategy, the reasons for any recent changes, and the meaning of market events that you uncover in the press.

In fact, use your functional expertise to identify important news from outside of your company and prepare topics of discussion before a meeting with someone whom you want to learn from. Bring some questions too, but keep them intensely relevant and listen for cues to stop a line of conversation that is draining enthusiasm. You don't need to prove how smart you are; you do need to prove that your smart brain is useful to the company.

D. BE ACCESSIBLE

With all of the above in place, accessibility is the only missing component. Whether or not you are accessible to your peers is a simple function of how you communicate, both verbally and nonverbally:

- Present yourself. Greet people you know, introduce yourself to those you don't. Look at people when you are speaking with them, and learn their names. Remind them of yours if you think they may not remember; soon enough, they will!

- Listen and don't interrupt. Write down things that are important, even if you believe you will not forget them. Keep a notebook handy and don't be afraid to pull it out any time.

- Respond to e-mail—but keep it clear and concise. Don't measure your words or stew over how to express it "just right." Nobody has time for long e-mails or to read complex meaning in them. If you want to create a policy statement that will be a permanent document, other media is more appropriate.

MIKE'S MANAGEMENT USE CASE

I admit it...I am horrible with names and faces. I have been embarrassed many times in my career because I did not recognize someone who clearly knew me. It has happened with customers, it has happened with coworkers, and frequently at company social events that include spouses. I have an intense feeling of failure when someone realizes that I don't know who they are. They either feel insulted by me, or they feel that I am a fool. Neither one of those outcomes is admirable.

I'm not proud of those times but I know it is a personal limitation and I try to recover from it with some special follow-on attention to the affected person. Like any mistake, I don't take it lightly but I also don't dwell on it and I try not to do it again. It would be far worse to hide and avoid situations altogether where I have to meet people.

You will face limitations of your own that result in repeated mistakes —perhaps more or less severe than mine. But the point is that you should not stop making an effort just because you fear failure. As long as you are gaining experience, even repetitive failures are preferable to inaction.

For all of the above, always *think.* Consider what you are saying and how it will be heard. What action will most likely be taken by the recipient as a result of your message? And is that the intended consequence of your communication? As a developer, you had to communicate a small amount of terse information only to your immediate team members. Bare facts were sufficient, even desirable. As a manager, the effects of what you communicate are extremely important. Many highly respected managers achieve their status by taking a little more time to consider one more level of ramifications before pressing "send."

E. LISTEN

Every one of the areas that will create willing followers involves listening. Every form of communication—spoken, nonverbal, e-mail—is an investment by someone to make an impression on you. If you disrespect this effort, you may not learn something important, and you will definitely lose a follower. Listen, reflect, and then respond thoughtfully. For emerging managers who have established a deep functional competency, this point cannot be emphasized enough. After years of being the *source* of technical communications, they have a hard time *keeping quiet.* Ironically, they are frustrated because they have neglected listening to the point that others will no longer communicate with them.

EMERGING MANAGER STEP SIX: SEEK COOPERATION

Many developers love to tackle difficult problems on their own. They work a problem from every angle in silent cubicles, springing forth after days or weeks with solutions that deserve the pride (or panic) that they show. These individuals are very productive and successful developers, but they are not demonstrating potential for leadership. An emerging manager solves problems with help from others, via consensus and communication—not without technical ability but with a different approach to overcoming hurdles between periods of productivity.

These hurdles, simple obstacles that dot the landscape of every programming task, are actually opportunities. When you encounter one, first *think* as any technical person would. Is it a problem that *can* be solved quickly? If not, use this as an opportunity to engage with your manager. Think of practical solutions—remember that management is common sense, so you have to show more than technical ability:

- Determine whether or not the obstacle is rooted in a real problem. For example, if it is due to a specific requirement, can that requirement be challenged and possibly rejected? Don't try to solve it just because it seems fun!

- If solving the problem is possible but it would be too costly or too risky, don't assume you should jump in and start doing it. Talk to the manager about it, pointing out the costs and risks, other activities that you could undertake instead and generally providing choices.

- Has anyone else solved a problem like it, and are they available to lend their solution to this problem too? Similarly, are there other groups working on similar problems now, and can they be consulted? If you have this information, make sure your manager has the chance to put it to use.

Write down alternatives, weighing the benefits and detriments of each. Then choose one and discuss it with your manager. In these exchanges you will be learning more about each other, and you will be creating a path for dialog that you will need when it's time to express concerns about your career.

The occasional communication with your manager may be one of the most important ways for you to make yourself visible within the organization. Consider three people:

- One who constantly escalates "unsolvable critical" problems

- One who reports good progress on projects and occasionally asks for help with a well-structured and constructive message

- One who doggedly and silently fights his way through a project without providing any visibility into what he does

Which one do you think will experience the fastest career growth? If you have good communication skills and you keep your work projects in order, you will soon find that you are being tapped to help the management team.

CLOSURE

A move onto the leadership track is not without effort. We've outlined quite a few things for you to start or continue doing as groundwork for a leadership position. But you would probably agree that none of those things are bad for you even if you don't make the leadership move. It turns out that being a great leader in software development starts with being a great software developer. When you are well underway with these initial steps, and the time is right for your next career change, you are ready to get moving.

———————

Chapter 4

GET MOVING

The mechanics of a management job may seem simple from your current vantage point—management tools, after all, are the mouse and microphone. In fact, starting a management job may look easier than it was to get the "hard" skills of a software developer. Management seems to require fewer specific skills and less concrete knowledge when compared to any sort of engineering, software, or otherwise.

Much of management wisdom is made up of simple rules and common sense. When you read management books or articles, you may find them absurdly trivial and even comical: full of messages like "people want praise and money" or "coaching improves a team." Laugh all you want, but then get serious because software management is a real discipline and it is being done very badly by many companies. You have an opportunity to do it well.

The core of the problem lies in the fact that companies and people, unlike machines, behave in widely differing and rather unpredictable ways. The genius of a Von Neumann Machine (all modern computers) is the ability to do simple things over and over again, very fast. But the genius of people is the opposite—we do complex things as few times as possible, with higher quality when we have more time to do them. It is also not so simple to motivate us to work. Electric power and machine language instructions will not do!

Managing people is very different from managing processors. Different skills (yes, those infamous "people skills" and many others) are required. They are not so hard to get once you know what you are looking for, but applying them correctly in a wide array of often ambiguous situations is challenging. Along the path, you may find that applying some of those management clichés is much harder to do than laughing at them.

Being *called* a team leader for the first time is about as hard as becoming a novice developer by typing PRINT "Hello World." But succeeding at your first leadership project may prove itself just as challenging as turning the first Hello World program into something useful, and you will learn just as much in the process. Newly obtained management knowledge and experience may not look impressive to the peers whom you are accustomed to impressing, but rest assured: the abilities you will be gaining are just as real.

All of this is not intended to intimidate or to persuade you that you are unqualified for the job. We are also not trying to take away the joy of mocking TV sitcom bosses or the camaraderie that builds when you discuss your manager's latest stunt with your friends at happy hour. But we want to give you a chance to realize that management is not nearly as trivial as it might appear. You almost certainly have the skills now that you need to *start* your career in management, but please dodge the pitfall assumption that you know *everything* about it. Stay humble and aware of the fact that you lack experience. You are much more likely to carefully analyze situations that way. And you may find that an open-minded probing approach lets you solve problems better than even a more experienced, but routine-oriented manager.

YOU HAVE TO ENTER TO WIN

In conjunction with the groundwork preparation that was discussed in the last chapter, you have to tackle the problem of finding a project to lead. One of the most obvious ways to do that is often overlooked: ask for it. Managers are constantly asked for compensation, or promotion, or equipment upgrades, or for improvements in the work schedule. What they don't often receive is someone volunteering to do more, to take on responsibility, to bridge a gap that is currently an unsolved problem for the business. Choose carefully what you ask for, and you will quickly have the assignment.

How you ask and what you ask for can make all the difference in the world. You have to offer yourself for a task that you could realistically complete, solving a business problem that is not already assigned to someone else. What you *can't* do is offer to solve a remote or minor problem with resources that are already assigned to a higher priority; doing so will just make you appear foolish. You also should not ask for more compensation or other recognition just because you start in a management role. That will come later when you prove that you can do it well.

> ### MIKE'S MANAGEMENT USE CASE
>
> When I was organizing a new department, I put a new manager in charge of a team of four people because he seemed eager to make a management move, and he had deep technical experience that would command respect. I felt certain that he would own his area of responsibility, doing whatever was necessary to succeed, and that I would have an easy time helping him learn the leadership ropes.
>
> He had only one request of me, which was that I promote him along with the role change. His last promotion was five years earlier, and I had only been managing people for about that long, so I did not know any better, and I agreed.
>
> That was a mistake. He was not ready to manage people, and he failed miserably even though he had the management title. I looked foolish for promoting him and he was rated poorly for not doing the job well. I misjudged his ability; he overstated his interest. Years later, he finally caught up and actually did the job that I promoted him into.

Even when they crave it, software developers will sometimes go to great lengths to avoid asking for leadership responsibility. Leadership hopes and dreams are only outwardly manifested as frustration and anxiety, cynicism and impatience. People who are otherwise objective will respond to management issues with bitter criticism and personal attacks. Those same people would never dream of polluting their technical reputation with subjective commentary.

An objective engineer does not want to criticize anyone in a less than constructive way. But because the nature of management problems is not a familiar domain, objectivity is sometimes hard to maintain. After all, identifying the problem is usually the biggest challenge in software debugging. Once correctly identified, the solution to a bug can take a thousand different forms. In management, the problem itself takes a thousand different forms—very different indeed.

FRIENDS IN ALL THE RIGHT PLACES

Many people make the mistake of assuming that career discussions are simpler with people who are personal friends— "having the boss over for dinner"—and the like. In reality, the professional conversations you can have with your manager or others in peer or superior roles are far more important to establish yourself as a strong candidate for leadership. You can still be friends too, but remember to keep your work and private life separate, and never compromise your leader with conflicting pressures.

HONZA'S MANAGEMENT USE CASE

I had a chance to hire and then manage a very close friend of mine. He brought strong talent and vast knowledge to the company, so I was always very happy with the decision to bring him on. But working with him presented a dilemma for me: I had to be particularly careful in any situation involving him so as not to arouse suspicion of nepotism.

Shortly after he was recruited, I made sure that he did not report directly to me, but rather through another manager in order to safeguard transparency. That worked well until a year later, when my friend was put up for promotion. My role was such that I had to approve or deny it. If you think it was an obvious decision, think again! I spent twice as much time thinking about his promotion as I spent on any other one at that time.

In the end, I approved the promotion. Now, years later, we no longer work closely together but my friend continues to take on ever bigger responsibilities and challenging projects, clearly proving that the promotion back then was justified. I feel very good about the time we worked together: he never got any preferential treatment but I do not think I hindered his progress either. It is very easy to do one or the other when you are the manager of a friend!

Responsible, ethical managers will always apply much more scrutiny to their close friends, or they will try to adjust the organization in such a way that they do not have to face a conflict of interests.

A FIRST PROJECT

Rarely will you have the chance to choose a brand new project with a hand-picked team. For one, you don't yet know how to choose a team, and two, you are not experienced enough to lead a project with the kind of priority that would empower you so highly. Don't argue for this kind of role; it's a non-starter. If the project idea is great, it will be handed to someone else; if it is not, it will just be ignored.

On the other hand, if you choose a project that is already up and running smoothly, you might think there's a good chance you'll be trusted to keep it going while you build up experience managing people, schedules, and so forth. This is a trap! Managing an established project has nothing but downsides for you:

- You won't be learning how to create a team (recruit complementary skills and attitudes, build esprit de corps, etc.)

- If the team does experience problems, you will be unprepared to deal with them and likely blamed for the downturn because the team was previously functioning.

- Assuming you do improve the overall team, you will probably share the credit with whoever preceded you, at best.

In short, there's no upside and plenty that can go wrong with an established, successful team.

MIKE'S MANAGEMENT USE CASE

An old friend who worked for another manager was given a first-time team lead role right about the middle of his career. He asked to speak with me and explained that he understood the role he was supposed to play, but that he could not just "turn over all those years of knowledge" to three new people (his new team) who would consequently make his own abilities obsolete. He also told me how bored he was with a job that never seemed to change much.

The irony was staring me in the face, but he did not even realize it. I told him to challenge himself to see how fast he could make his team productive. His responsibility would be to move from one person to the next, clearing obstacles and enabling them to do a better job, faster. As a person who would multiply the productivity of each of the people on his team, I explained that his new role was more valuable to the company than his old one. I asked him if he really believed that someone could be trained in just a few months to do the job he had learned in half a career.

Finally, I asked him if he would like to clear the backlog of work that was piled up a year deep on his plate and maybe even take a vacation without a pager. Within a week, he was a great new team lead for three eager people who will probably remember him for the rest of their professional lives.

TOO HOT, TOO COLD…JUST RIGHT

A great kind of project to help emerging managers build real skills is something that's already in *trouble*. *Chronic* trouble is even better. It has to be important enough to require a fix but not so important that the business hinges on it. It has to have some level of personnel assigned and a reasonable profile. This kind of project has minimal downside for you:

- You will be virtually guaranteed to learn from it because it has obvious problems to fix. You will be overwhelmed at how fast tough issues will be put on you just because you stepped into the breach. Whether that's clients, deadlines, people, requirements, process, budget, or other difficulties, you will be unfamiliar with them, and you will have to learn how to solve them without writing code. And yes, that is good news!

- If you are not successful, no one will be surprised. You are not expected to succeed. In fact, most people will wonder why you wanted to work on a troubled project at all. "Of course, it failed; it was headed there the whole time."

- You won't have to work hard to get assigned this role. You can probably volunteer for it, and maybe agree to take on management of it part-time while you are still working on something else.

- If it is not working out, you can probably make a quick exit back to your previous role without a whole lot of collateral damage. However, if you are no longer needed in your previous role, you may not have that retreat path, so be sure before you make a move.

- You will be left alone—the solution won't be spoon-fed to you by someone higher in management. You will be free to make unorthodox and rookie mistakes because other managers will have little at stake in your success or failure.

- Any improvement you make will be noticed and credited to you—and if you have avoided just coding your way out of the problem, you will have a great time explaining what you did and why it worked. Make sure you have something interesting to say!

- If you do succeed, you won't be stuck on this project. You'll be too useful already to stay on something that was allowed to flounder for a long time before you. In the worst case, you'll move on to something else that has a similar profile where you can make another impressive mark. In the best case, you'll keep this responsibility and take on more projects somewhere else.

If it's so easy, why doesn't everyone do it? First, because it is not intuitive that as a great developer with a bright future on the next hot project, you would drop back and choose to be on *that* team. *That* team seems to be full of people who are not as adept as others and their careers are not moving. *That* team is not part of what the press releases are about and their cachet is nonexistent.

And second, because it is not *so easy*! The team or project is in trouble for some reason. It may not be trivial to understand the root cause(s) of the problem, and it may be even harder to implement the solution. But that is exactly the type of challenge through which you will learn and grow.

A word of caution is needed here. If you do choose to join a team with chronic issues, and if you then choose to use your own grunt as a developer to fix the problems, you will be in the worst possible situation. First, you won't have proven anything about your management skills. Second, you will have alienated the people on the team that you joined, and these people may one day work for you. Third, you may be stuck in this role until you find an equally qualified developer to take it over. On the other hand, if you used management efforts to fix it, you're probably OK because the company will just ask you to transition whatever you did to a new manager.

EARLY LEADERSHIP DO'S AND DON'TS

Don't Compete Against Your Peers. Working against a peer is the wrong place to focus your energy. Unfortunately, it is a very real phenomenon that is fomented by misguided leaders. Every company has far too many needs for leaders and far too few leaders to fill them, so there is no need to compete for one specific management role. As a future manager, you need every possible resource aligned with you and your goals. You should consider *everyone* to be someone that you may need to lead at some point in time.

If you feel you are in competition for a knowledge-based leadership role, find a compromise as fast as you can. Taking the side of someone you disagree with is a great way to show that you are supportive of your peers, you are flexible in approach, and you are willing to compromise.

Conflict is a form of turmoil that signals when it is a good time to effect change. As you develop yourself, few people will notice the gradual changes in your approach. Your peers will require a cathartic event to realize that the new *you* is different and operating at a new level. Managing conflict and difficult situations is a primary role of a manager, so you will want to build this ability. Use competitive situations to work toward a resolution that is optimal for the business and show that you are a leader.

Do Put Your Team First. Something that surprises many new managers is that they actually work *for* their team, not the other way around. The manager is successful only if everyone on the team is:

- Satisfied with the level of challenge and growth of the work assigned to them

- Comfortable with the pressures of delivery

- Fully equipped with tools, labs, communication lines, etc.

- Fully informed of the schedule, work, and delivery plan

- Trained and competent in the skills required to complete the task

That's a lot of work! Even a small team of three people is a substantial amount of work for a new manager, especially because the "first level" manager directly leading a small team has to be involved in the greatest amount of detail. Sometimes team members are easy to manage and the project is easy to segment and execute—but that's usually not true except in college courses!

In the real world, the manager is constantly making decisions about how to overcome obstacles, prioritize efforts, and evaluate risks. Successful leadership by a great manager can appear, from the team's perspective, to be a magical power because the manager seemingly knows the future when he or she accurately predicts what is going to happen. The truth is, of course, that experience is a great teacher. The same organized mind that once designed programs or found software bugs by thinking through the execution of code can also be trained to recognize patterns in far more complex systems consisting of clients, organization dynamics, and market swings.

MIKE'S MANAGEMENT USE CASE

One of the most nontechnical managers I know diagnosed several technical problems, to my astonishment, during my early career. He had simply learned to link symptoms with major subsystems through years of practice even though he did not know how or why the subsystems would cause such problems. Similarly, I was once given a tour of a research facility by an apparent super genius, who turned out to be a twenty-year veteran of daily facility tours—with no formal training! If these things can happen when non-technical people pay attention to what is happening in the technical arena, imagine what you can do if you don't tune out the management side of things at your company!

Don't Hide Bad News; Do Offer Solutions. Leadership, and specifically software development management, is about facing every challenge head-on. Many such challenges will come and go without ever being reported outside of your team. But when new *big* problems are found, don't try to hide them. It is far better to assess the situation and communicate about what is happening. Specifically, you need to determine:

- That the problem is real

- What the possible solutions might be

- What you need from management to address it

That's the approach that will win you respect because it shows that your abilities will scale to ultimately solve any problem in the business. Trying to solve it on your own or hiding it in hopes of making it go away will not pay off in the long run.

Remember that the scope of the solution has to match the scope of the problem—you usually won't be successful asking for twice the initial budget or massive delays right before the deadline. That kind of request will put your leaders in an awkward position of having to reject your ideas without a lot of discussion—there's no point in listening to your arguments if your ideas cannot be implemented practically. Yes, it is possible that a project needs a massive reset, but you are probably not yet qualified to handle that large of a management problem.

MIKE'S MANAGEMENT USE CASE

A customer once hacked in to my product and maliciously harmed his employer. He then proceeded to contact the CTO of his company to report that my products were not safe, that he had proof of it in the form of the damage he had done, and that my company should be fired at once. Instead of doing what he asked, his company fired him and prosecuted him legally for his malicious actions.

I have to assume that this individual meant well but the solution that he proposed (get rid of my product) was not proportional to the problem that he wanted to solve (fix the security holes). He completely missed the idea that his company was solving many different problems with my product and therefore could not simply abandon us because of some minor defects. This misunderstanding happens all the time in the management world but you can avoid it. Just remember that any solution you propose has to be considered as part of the entire project it fits into, not just the small piece that currently holds your attention.

Do Learn from Everything You Do. Get a mentor to critique you—think of feedback as a mirror for your abilities. Don't even think about being defensive against the criticism but instead choose the portion of it that you *can* change. Then do it and go back for more. You might encounter a mental block here: you have to thirst for criticism to help you grow. When you do get some well-thought-out feedback, write it down and absorb it slowly, working to understand why you do what you do, and then change the fundamentals that will make you better. View management as a theatrical performance—a role to learn, and eventually to master.

If you are insufficiently analytical, commit to spending 20 minutes in thought during your busy schedule each day. If you are not informed sufficiently, commit two hours a week to getting up to speed on whatever the key area may be. If you cannot speak in public, join a club that helps people like you, or sign up for a night course in communications. The important thing is to take an active, short-term approach to improvement. Don't spend too much time making a big plan for an MBA or even a two week seminar sometime far in the future when you can immediately begin making progress now.

Read. The fact that you have this in front of you is the result of a willingness to grow. There is a wealth of information for you to learn from. It is important to realize that there is always a hot new business book out there, and it is probably on the desk of a few people at your company now. Find out what it is and read it. You may understand some or all of the concepts. But you will also learn the current vernacular of management science—terms like "Red Ocean" (from *Blue Ocean Strategy*) or phrases like "Great is the enemy of good" (from *Good to Great*).

MIKE'S MANAGEMENT USE CASE

I inherited a team with a lead who had tripped into the leadership role when his manager retired with no succession plan. The team was stable and the product was in reasonable shape as far as customers were concerned, so I thought it would be simple to add them into my responsibilities.

The first time we sat down to formally review active development projects, I was inundated by a long list of "almost complete" efforts. Most of them were ready to go to clients, but no client actually wanted them. The lead had diligently tasked eight people for four months with work that was completely unnecessary when we examined the commercial (profit) motives.

Processes were followed and quality was very high. But he had never actually talked to product managers or clients, or anyone else who had an external perspective. When I forced the issue of engaging people from outside of product development, we learned that the product was in fact on a severe decline due to competitive technologies that were disrupting the marketplace. The product had become a laggard. The only viable solution was to stop investing in the laggard solution and place the effort elsewhere.

The manager was demoted, and de-motivated, but he regained his foothold as a technical expert soon thereafter, and learned a big lesson in leadership. In the process, I nearly lost him and all of his knowledge to another company because I was so heavy handed in my management approach. I had the right goal (practical, effective teams) but the wrong style ("my way, or the highway"). He saw through my lack of management experience and actually helped me adjust to a more moderate approach while still achieving my goals, even though the outcome was not going to be positive for him. Learning opportunities for new managers happen when you least expect them!

YOUR VALUABLE PERSPECTIVE

One of the most valuable tools that a new development manager has in his or her arsenal is the ability to recall all too recently what it was like to face the challenges that he or she now must ask others to face. For example, most professional software engineers have been asked to complete seemingly impossible tasks during a "crunch time" for their teams. These are situations where schedule or technology barriers appear to make the goal of the team either impossible or impractical.

Great managers who evaluate these situations correctly are actually expecting the chaotic dynamics of complex software projects and plan to use them toward some unpredictable but positive outcome. They know that getting stuck in "analysis paralysis" is as bad as not analyzing at all. Changes in the requirements are all too familiar—that's what happens, frequently, in the software engineering world. Some of the most difficult problems are simply abandoned because of lucky changes in requirements. And, of course, sometimes the worst defect turns out to be a feature because customers like the odd unintended side effect of a mistake. What other discipline faces that sort of incongruity?

Emerging managers have some knowledge of the technical ramifications of every change, defect, or ripple in the project, so they are not worried that a goal is fundamentally unattainable. They don't specifically know how it will be attained, but they can count on the evolution of the solution in favorable but unpredictable ways as the schedule unfolds. It is like a good sailor heading out to sea, confident of some means of return, even when the power source is as random as the weather. The uncertainty would crush anyone trying to *manage* software without ever having built it. But the knowledge of the emerging manager empowers very fortuitous arbitrage—what seems like a large technical risk to the untrained eye is understood and even used advantageously by a great developer who has the reins.

CLOSURE

This chapter reviewed some basic patterns of behavior which will identify you as a rational and open minded leader who puts the success of the team ahead of his or her own benefit. We also discussed how to find your first opportunity to emerge as a manager—the right team or project where you can add a lot of value and learn to lead. Surprisingly, that first opportunity is often one of the more problematic projects or teams at your company! Regardless of what you lead, your job is about to change. The chapters ahead will help you sort it out and succeed.

———————

Chapter 5

GOALS

One of the first things you will realize when you look at management from the *manager's* side is that the goals set for you, like never before in your career, appear to be opposing each other:

Goal	Opposing Goal
Stay on budget and on time	Don't burn out any team members
Get the job done well	Complete the job as cheaply as possible
Build team spirit	Build healthy competition within the team to get higher productivity
Increase the skills of the team	Use only expert resources to avoid risk and training costs
Learn to manage people	Help get the work done yourself

The heart of this apparent contradiction is the ambiguous challenge faced at every level of management: short-term results vs. long-term progress. You have to get the work done now but also set your team up for greater, unknown work that will come later. Grappling with the duality of these goals is awkward and confusing. Get the most out of the team, but don't burn them out. The deadline is critical but vacations must be approved. There's no time for training but there are some brand new tools and techniques that could speed the project along. The very best managers understand this well. You will have to hone the ability to gauge when to emphasize immediate needs or when to lay a foundation for the future. You have to optimize progress against two conflicting goals, knowing that neither will be fully met.

A technical career presents many problems that require a satisfactory outcome for conflicting goals. But even the most ambiguous technical problem is typically better defined and more quantifiable than the challenges you will face daily in management. It is a good environment to learn in because every action that you plan must be preceded by a thought exercise in which you weigh its impact on all of your goals. Later on, when your compensation is leveraged by bonuses that pay out based on goal achievement, you will feel this balance even more clearly.

Until you can navigate decisions that pit short- and long-term results (strategic vs. tactical, profit vs. growth, etc.) against each other, you will be uneasy and you will lack confidence in your ability to manage. You won't necessarily be doing a bad job of managing, but it will simply be uncomfortable. That's OK! Harness the unease into attention to detail. The great news is that when you do master it, this ability will continue to serve you in larger and larger scopes of management need. That's because all of management, all the way to the top job in the biggest company, is about planning what is to be done now in order to achieve a greater result later. It sounds easy, but most of the time, it goes wrong!

MANAGEMENT GONE BAD, OR SETTING UP TO WIN?

You're probably familiar with the adage that mistakes discovered early are many times cheaper to correct than ones addressed later on. The same principle applies to your success in leadership: how you initiate a project, what goals you establish and how you align people and resources against those goals will all have a great impact on the project outcome much later on.

	Resources Assigned Incorrectly	Resources Assigned Correctly
Goals Set Incorrectly	The wrong people, both management and technical, are asked to do impractical things. The effort is doomed from the start.	A great team is given a hopeless goal. They might pull it off, but at what cost?
Goals Set Correctly	A great and worthy goal given to the wrong team: good people mismatched for the role or poor performers doomed to fail.	The classic win-win situation. A capable team is given a goal that is worth achieving. Hard work will be rewarded with a worthwhile result.

BREAKING IT DOWN

The solution to every goal you face as a lead or manager involves two components: a problem *scope* and a resource *constraint*. On one hand, your job is to understand the problem scope inside and out—all the nuances of priority and technology, all the history and the specifics of the starting point. On the other hand, you have to understand the team and what they are capable of doing, how you want each of them to grow during this project and how you want to grow yourself.

Taking this a step further, one set of results that is expected from you is provided in neatly documented goals for the project and team—oftentimes, you will be asked to write these goals after discussions with your leaders. These are called different things in different environments, but we call them *program* goals and you report on them formally, periodically, in *program* reviews. On the other hand, another set of goals, the ones that will demonstrate your mastery of management to everyone around you, are what we call *meta*-results. Some examples of meta-results are:

- Build better technical skills on your team

- Build better management skills for you and for others on your team

- Build a working team that can be productive in the future by taking on the next challenge, supporting each other because they know each other's skills and commitment, they have built esprit de corps, interpersonal chemistry, and relationships

- Extend the technical base of the company

- Build some reusable (documented, published) components

> **MIKE'S MANAGEMENT USE CASE**
>
> I was less than a year into my career when suddenly I had the chance to work on a cool new product. I still had to get my normal work done but if I would stay after-hours and come in on weekends, then I could be part of a team that was doing something new and interesting. I was ready for the challenge and soon our small team scheduled a first demonstration of what we had done.
>
> We practiced carefully, tested all night, and finally it was time for the meeting with a mid-level exec who could either allow us to continue our "side project," or shut it down for good. I felt like I was glowing when the demonstration started. I never knew work could be so much fun. I was sure we would get the green-light to work on the new product full-time.
>
> After about 3 minutes of the demo, the exec turned to someone else that he had invited to the meeting and said "Has anyone taken a serious look at this?" They exchanged a few phrases, after which they both got up, and left.

I was humiliated, embarrassed and frustrated. In a word, I was destroyed. Did that exec really think that our work was not serious? Looking back on it now, I know that he meant "Has anyone looked at the full project cost to develop and sell this, compared to the risk, market size and competitive threats?" No one had taken that kind of serious look at it because we were too busy having fun with technology. He expected profit projections, we brought a prototype; meeting concluded.

The outcome was appropriate and the situation taught me several lessons (pay attention to the business case, set expectations before meetings, etc.). But that exec could have achieved the same result while still preserving the dignity of the people in the room. He caused a lot of collateral damage for the company and his own career.

Program goals are the first priority—without getting the commercial result desired by the company, you will disappoint everyone no matter how much your team learns or what tools they build for others to use. But if, in the process of achieving commercial goals, you can also advance the people and products, so that future results are more efficiently attainable, then you are a *great* manager. On the other hand, if your approach is that "the end justifies the means" and your program goal success actually destroys future potential for the company, you need to place some serious focus on why you have chosen management as a career.

Program Goals and Meta-Results Examples	Meta-Damage	Meta-Results
Poor Results on Program Goals	Your team delivered a low-quality product that is late, even though everyone is burned out from overworking while trying to get it done; now the best people on your team are job hunting. This is the worst-case scenario: you have mismanaged the team and the project. You may be much more successful on a technical career track if you find yourself in this position more than a few times!!	For example, if the product is late but it includes some fundamental components that will be reused on future projects, and team members learn each other's strengths and have begun to rely on each other, thinking ahead about how they can interlock abilities to deliver stronger results next time. If you delivered very late or very low quality, you risk being considered too academic and unfocussed. Remember, program goals are essential.
Great Results on Program Goals	You patched a legacy system to achieve functionality on time and on budget, but the skills your team used are not useful any longer. Consider the principal areas of meta-results (people and career development, creating reusable foundations, future extensions of your work) and look at specific ways to improve your approach to each and every one next time.	You deliver high quality, on time, including baseline goals and stretch goals for the product. And in doing so, you prepared a technical leader for a management role in the future and trained two junior team members on tools so that they are now up for technical track promotion. Congratulations. YOU are going to have a fantastically successful management career.

META-DAMAGE

The concept of *meta* damage applies to impacts you have on the product, people, or company, which are not immediately adverse but which create a "long shadow" of repercussions. Make no mistake—meta damage is real, and it can ruin apparent success for new managers. When your team is de-motivated or a key person leaves your business, a new manager might be inclined to rationalize the problem and attribute it to external factors. But the reality is that the manager's role is to care for and to develop every resource entrusted to him or her. Nothing related to the team is outside the manager's concern. There are many forms of meta-damage that you may not feel responsible for but which you will ultimately be held responsible:

- Long-term under-performing team members. Aside from being dissatisfied themselves, having a team member who is an under-performer is highly disappointing to rest of the team—especially the strongest members of the team. The manager has to deal with performance issues straight-on, regardless of the age or experience difference between manager and team member. Every project is an opportunity to correct a personnel problem, no matter how long the problem has been tolerated by other managers. If you perpetuate a problem rather than solving it, you are destroying future results. See this as a chance to learn and tackle it!

- Violations of company architecture, process, etc. Certainly, it's true that rules are made to be broken, and doing so will sometimes save money and time with no adverse effects. But breaking rules as a matter of course without regard for the aftershocks will at the very least create a low perception of your team, it will build an attitude of nonconformance among your team members, and it will cause lower quality or usability in the long run. Get educated about the rules and follow them. If you don't like them, work to change them, but follow what's in place.

- Delivering low quality to end users. Customers, whether internal or external, will clamor for you to finish, potentially putting a lot of pressure on you and on your leaders. But when you deliver a poor product, the harm is far worse than would have come from a delay. The same people who desperately wanted the product will quickly claim that they would have been willing to wait if they knew it was *that* bad. Stick to your quality processes (or fix them) and don't deliver poor solutions. It's bad to be late, but it's much worse to have low quality from the customer's perspective. Work hard to understand what is acceptable to your users and deliver something they will accept.

- Burdening future projects with leftover personnel or product problems. You can't commit future features in the product or future promotions for team members. Similarly, you can't create dead-end products that cannot later be expanded or exhaust people who are going to be in critical need for intense projects immediately after your project ends. Keep all of your commitments aboveboard and documented, whether that's vacation time or refactoring to-dos that were postponed. Discuss these openly as a precondition to your results—not as an afterthought. Once you dispense the "candy," which is the results of your team, you won't be able to get stakeholders to meet commitments in return that they did not previously know about.

Even for the most eagerly emerging manager, this all may seem complex and unattainable. So much is prescribed—scope of work, duration, team members—it seems that the manager is just boxed-in to an administrative oversight role. And the only way to stand out is to achieve even more complex results, including things like career development for team members and system architecture improvements for the product. Yet you probably know someone who is a great manager and does all of that—but how?

MIKE'S MANAGEMENT USE CASE

A whole book has probably been written somewhere about how to know when software is ready to be released. The fact is that it depends on many things; resolving it will pull together all possible stakeholders. How urgently do customers need the product? Are they willing to deal with the known issues? Are there many unknown issues (because you are still finding new ones, or you are not testing well enough)? How fast can you react when problems are found?

So then I asked how much longer it would be before the quality assurance team could assure the quality of the product. The answer still shocks me..."Since QA did not create the software, we cannot certify it." After a few more circular answers, I decided I was getting nowhere so I dove into the testing records. The QA team had done a stellar job and the product was ready. We released the software, and it was fine.

The manager's role is to accept responsibility and to take calculated risks delivering. When the QA manager refused the responsibility because of the risk, she limited her own ability to grow into future roles.

SETTING UP TO SCORE A POINT

The answer is at the heart of one of those seemingly obvious management clichés: get set up to win. Of course you will succeed if you are "set up" for success. But that's a misunderstanding of the cliché—it actually refers to you, as a manager, doing the "setting up" work. It's the team that is "set up" and will therefore win because of what *you* do. It's the company that is "set up" and will therefore win because of the future successes that *you* empower.

You have responsibility for taking an active role understanding and moving each of the constraints placed on you—people, scope, time, and other resources (sometimes people are called human resources; this is a gross oversimplification of the value of people vs.

objects or space so avoid it when talking to the team). You are accustomed to technical challenges laid out in specifications or stated in concrete terms. The reality is that management tasks are *softer*. If there is no flexibility in terms of who you have on the team, how long you have to deliver, or what you are delivering then you have no room to evaluate and decide on necessary adjustments to achieve the goals. Therefore, you would have little room to *manage*. You would be *unempowered* in management parlance.

As a developer, you would have perceived an insurmountable barrier created by these constraints; most often you would not have enough information to know what had to be done and which parts were somewhat arbitrary. As a manager, your job is just as much to take down the barrier as it is to climb it.

The bottom line is that management is about creating change. You will gain empowerment very slowly, and only if you use it responsibly to change small things. And because most changes that you make will impact other teams, your changes have to be planned for the benefit of everyone—your team, other teams, the company as a whole. If the management team does not work in unison on decisions related to dates, scope, and people, then a great deal of damage can be done by a single poor manager.

As a new manager, you can't have the flexibility to make *big* decisions, but you are expected to suggest and drive *small* ones. If your suggestions are good (because they provide results and meta-results), then your authority to make decisions will grow along with the team size that you manage. On the other hand, if you are too timid, choosing not to implement any changes or asking permission at each step, then you will limit your own growth as a manager.

MIKE'S MANAGEMENT USE CASE

A well-intentioned team lead was doing a great job of communicating with his people: setting goals, praising, and so forth. After a round of good results, he wanted to recognize some of his team so he asked for permission to purchase a small gift certificate that he could present along with a short accolade.

His manager asked him to write a justification for the gift certificate expense, which he did. But there was no formal review process for this sort of reward, and the manager was not informed sufficiently to make a determination about whether to grant or deny the request. So the request sat unanswered until the "moment" was lost—the team lead who requested the award did not want to recognize an accomplishment from so long ago without also addressing other accomplishments that had happened since.

The team lead was very frustrated, essentially feeling unempowered because of the company bureaucracy. In reality, he should have just gone ahead and purchased the gift certificate (and gotten reimbursed via an expense report). The amount was about the same as one hour of his salary; the company entrusted him to decide how to spend a lot more than that every day. Many management tasks require improvisation and creative extensions to established practices. He became frustrated and unfortunately left the company.

It is important to look for small improvements continuously. Identify decisions you could make to fix problems with people, products, the workplace, processes, etc. Gather the correct information to make decisions, and make them confidently, with integrity, logic, and transparency. Later on, after a certain level of experience and loyalty has been created among willing followers, a certain tolerance for mistakes will be allowed. But early on, mistakes can be difficult to overcome—not in terms of reversing the decision but in terms of the collateral damage.

GRAPPLING WITH RESOURCE DECISIONS

When you begin taking hold of this power, initiating change, you will encounter the challenge of making and defending resource decisions. Very simple questions such as where people will sit or how equipment should be distributed can become the subject of intense debate unless decisions are made objectively with rationale that can be laid before the whole team to challenge. Even though no one thought of changing anything before you suggested it, everyone will have an opinion once you set the idea in motion!

Logical, comprehensive, and completely unbiased decisions by the manager will end the debate and get resources set once again in motion, hopefully in an optimized configuration. On the other hand, biased, political, or simply arbitrary, uninformed decisions will spark controversy and discontent, stopping progress. Many of the people you manage will desire an outcome that is not optimal for the whole team—whether they know it or not. Someone will disagree with every decision you make. But when you make a good overall choice and stick to it, everyone will gain respect for you.

EMPOWERING YOURSELF—SCOPE, TEAM, AND TIME

Most software development environments will have too much work scheduled for a given team and time frame. That's where the cliché "Good, Fast, or Cheap—Pick two" originates. It literally implies that a development manager cannot achieve complete deliverables of high quality in a short time. The manager, therefore, has to choose which elements of the work can most likely be delayed, which ones can be limited to minimal implementation, and which ones can be of lowest quality. A whole book could be written about that!

While the cliché is careless and cavalier, it is undeniable that a good manager will consider options impacting cost, time, and quality (defined here as the feature level of the product, not "bug density") as part of being empowered to set up a winning team. Those are, after all, the output variables that are under your control. Optimizing for all three of them at once is as creative an art as any engineering design ever was.

The key is to strive mercilessly toward a simpler and simpler answer to the most basic goal-oriented question: how are we going to succeed?

Your plan as a manager should be always to look out for trouble ahead, or ways to improve, and to cherish these problems when you find them. After all, if there were no problems, there would be no need for management, and having problems that have not yet been found is far worse than knowing what they are. Another cliché—"It's not a problem, it's an opportunity"—is right after all. It is an opportunity to learn, to communicate, to improve, or to drive better results. It is an opportunity for you to demonstrate judgment when you propose decisions that are bigger than your current responsibility and the reasons why.

There is a mindset change that is required here. You are accustomed to getting a problem and tearing into it. Now you have to make a habit of searching out problems and delegating them. In fact, you can never get stuck on one issue; you must find more problems. Worse yet, you are accustomed to finding problems and working to overcome them *by yourself* before resorting to others. As a manager, you should engage more people, rather than fewer. Your very instinct to power through problems can be deadly if you let it turn you inward rather than remaining an outward communicator.

Team members expect a lot from the manager. It's one of the harder parts of being a technical manager—you have to keep up with the commercial-minded management team and the technically minded development team. You will make mistakes—maybe in both areas! Be ready to take comfort in the lessons you learn rather than finding despair in management failures. Be ready to say you are sorry and reverse decisions that were made poorly. But most of all, be ready to stay in the game. Don't expect perfection from yourself and don't let team members challenge your authority just because you were not born a manager.

Any problem that can be solved using your company's standard practices or your team's engineering processes is just part of daily work. It's the new problems or the unconventional solutions that will define your creativity as a great manager. Just exactly how you propose to solve such problems is crucially important:

- You have to demonstrate that you fully understand the obstacle and proposed solution, and you have considered any other changes that should be implemented beforehand.

- You have to demonstrate that you know how your solution will impact all stakeholders—your team, other teams, clients, marketing, etc.

- You have to demonstrate that the results you get from overcoming the obstacle are deterministic and more aligned with success than the current plan.

- You must have done all that you can on your own within your responsibility before proposing that other teams are impacted.

If you are entering a leadership role over a team that has had many leaders in recent times, the best approach is to *show* rather than *say*. Often, troubled projects or products will cycle through a few different leaders as management struggles to find the right solution to the leadership problem. When it's your turn, you have a good chance of failing simply because everyone before you did too and the team members expect you to fail. They will be outright cynical toward any idea you propose. When this happens, the most effective approach we have found is to avoid over advertising your plans but steadily and consistently implement them in small pieces over time. When communicating openly, state that your plan is to prove results before you propose change; in other words, it's business as usual with you as the boss. When working with individuals who can be transformed by your efforts one at a time, initiate small changes to the environment without linking them into a broader pattern. After about six weeks, you will look like a genius who stabilized the team and moved it into a productive structure.

OVERCOMING OBSTACLES TO SUCCESS: SCOPE

You want to be successful with your project. That means that you want to achieve the business goal that the project is trying to address. No one will remember whether you developed all of the items that you had in your project plan, but everyone will remember whether the client was or was not happy in the end (and how successful the product was in the marketplace).

Emerging managers who are recently mined from technical ranks have a tendency to clearly "box in" what they are supposed to achieve. They feel that there are many things that are out of their control (it's true, there are such things, but not as many as you think), and therefore they want to anticipate failure by saying very explicitly that they will deliver, for example, A, B, and C.

Not more, not less. That way, if the team is asked to do more than A, B, and C, the manager feels like that prior warning is a "get out of jail" card. It is an easy way to push responsibility for the success of the project away, reducing the manager's job to something like operations management:

Operations Management	Team Management
Make sure people are working enough and paid correctly	Make sure the work they are doing is effective and appropriate
Make sure equipment is working properly	Make sure we have the right equipment and people are using it correctly
Make sure the status reports are turned in on time	Make sure the status reports are accurate
Make sure that someone wants to buy the product before we build it	Make sure the product is excellent at its purpose so it will sell

The difference in these columns should be clear. There is a definite need for each focus. But team management has a lot more integration with the people and the projects than operations management. Defining the scope tightly may provide an operations management framework but will leave you stranded when you need options with your team. Think of narrowly defined scope as a reduction in the number of corrective actions you can make later on. There are many ways to solve any business problem—some more complex, some simpler. A great management rule of thumb is this: *define the problem well, define the solution loosely*.

In this way, your team's objectives will remain clear, but you will have some latitude to implement a larger or smaller solution.

To explain this further, imagine that you diligently nail down the detailed scope of an effort, only to realize halfway through the project that you are not going to be able to finish. You will not be able to compromise on quality because a poor delivery will be a failure for you and your team. You can do your best to motivate productivity (incentives, pep talks, hands-on help, and advice). But you can't shift the detailed scope because that's part of how you defined your success. If, on the other hand, you have some level of latitude, it is very likely that you and your team (remember to get them involved) will be able to come up with alternative implementations that will salvage the schedule and the goals. That's a far better option than failing alto-gether!

MANAGING UP—COMMUNICATING CHANGES IN SCOPE

You have a brilliant idea. It's going to save time and money. Your team will love it. You feel like you're finally on top of the management game. Now you just have to convince someone above you, so you can actually do it.

Or maybe you have a problem. You are predicting de-lays or quality trouble, unforeseen complications, etc. You need help, but you're not sure you understand the problem. Once again, you have to discuss it with some-one above you.

MIKE'S MANAGEMENT USE CASE

I was the product development manager for a small group, reporting to a business manager who had no technical experience. I was brought in to the role because the team was failing before I arrived. Once I learned who was on the team and their strengths, I reorganized the projects, and productivity improved in about three months. However, each time I would leave the office for a few days (vacation, business trips), I would return to a distressed environment. While I was away, the business manager would contact various people in the product development team and change their priorities away from our well-organized project schedule.

On my return, he would apologize but claim that whatever he had changed was absolutely necessary. Inevitably, we would discuss the changes and his reasons for each of them, only to discover that nothing should have been altered in my absence after all, because I understood all of his priorities and included them in my plan.

After about the third time that all of his orders were reversed when I returned, the development team stopped reacting to his short-term direction when I went away. They understood why their projects were important and why other distractions were not. Your company needs for you to be the manager because you will do a better job—often that will mean that you disagree with other

> managers above you. But remember, that's why they need you, so don't cave in.

Whenever you have a responsibility and you are interacting with someone of greater responsibility, always propose solutions along with the issues you raise. Provide choices, the most practical ones possible. Here are some tricks—maybe these have been used by your managers in the past, maybe they will only now become clear to you. In all cases, these are communication and persuasion tools, not misrepresentations of fact:

- Understand what is being asked of the team and eliminate portions of it that do not directly contribute to the organization's goal. For example, a requirement to create a database replication mechanism is a broad statement of a "real" problem, which is to synchronize two tables between two databases. Often the requirements are written in a general form assuming that the implementation will be such that it can be reused on other projects. If the reuse is a stated part of the goal, and you have the right people, then don't ask to remove it. But if you know how your portion of the effort fits into a broader project and the general reuse is not useful, then you can ask to constrain the goals and ensure your success.

- Deliver a project in stages, not as one "big bang." If the project is known to be at some risk already, odds are you can get away with incremental deliverables, showing progress along the way. The first stage, which by definition does not include all of the requirements, is delivered on the required schedule. This is often something that clients can understand and will respond well to because they would like to receive incremental deliverables. But make sure each stage proves some level of technical feasibility that packs "punch" into your work. People who depend on you need to be able to see demonstrated results of each stage.

- Identify the level of effort behind each part of the goal and show a list of the parts with a "cutoff line," below which appear things that cannot be accomplished on the required schedule. Give yourself some room when you start this conversation (i.e., place the cutoff line a little higher than it needs to be), assuming that you will have to bargain down with your manager.

- Approach team members and ask which portions of the project they are passionate about. Then assign them these parts (assuming they are competent to complete the work) and *overload* what is required of them precisely because you are leveraging their passion. Then, when you speak to your manager, it will be clear that each team member is well utilized and your argument will be simpler. When you speak to your team members, you are doling out the technical authority to complete the work, not just a task list.

- Find an existing commercial product that solves a part of the problem you are being asked to solve. When you discuss this with superiors, note that other suppliers have identified a subset of the functionality as a stand-alone commercial product. Therefore, your company could choose to purchase rather than build that part of the solution. Even if a purchase is not possible (because, for example, the other supplier is a rival competitor), your superiors may be forced to acknowledge that you are being asked to achieve more than they had anticipated.

- Ask for interns or trainees to work on your project with you. Choose carefully and you will have productive resources that you did not expect.

- Always reflect a level of confidence with your projections. For example, you could state that it is possible to achieve the goal with the resources provided, but you are facing unknowns in certain areas outside your control (list them) and therefore the uncertainties lead to risk. Commit to managing this risk over time, but use the uncertainties and the need to manage them as a means to request more resources. Bring these up each time you are asked to provide an update on the project. Be careful not to "hedge" by saying that you won't be responsible for whatever happens. You are responsible, and you would like to reduce the risks you foresee in your delivery.

- Seek incentives for the team based on the required level of effort. Set expectations high for what is needed, then manage very carefully and always keep some time or effort in reserve.

NOT TO DO'S

You are not expected to do all of the things listed above as a new manager, but understanding them will be to your advantage like having a roadmap before discovering a new place. Using the same analogy, it might be useful to know what not to do as well—ways to stay out of trouble as you learn your way. Here are a few simple things *not to do* when you are provided a challenge:

- Say that the goal is impossible

- Ask to have more people added to your team without justification or background information

- Panic, freeze, and fail to lead your team

- Try to redirect the goals by saying the program is not needed or the business mission is wrong

MIKE'S MANAGEMENT USE CASE

You will often think that the goals of your company are set wrong. Maybe you think a certain product is not needed, or a technology is too outdated to be propagated any further. Don't ignore that instinct, but before you escalate a problem, think your team will ask you. The worst thing you can about it long and hard. Examine it from other people's perspectives and try to get complete information.

If it still does not make sense, even after a few days of churning, take it up with your boss. You may find out that you were missing some important information. It is your right to ask—because do is to say, "I do not know why we are supposed to do this, and I don't really think we should, but let's get it done." If you don't believe in the work, you have a high chance of failing!

Once I left a large company because my instinct told me they were working on a completely mis-guided product line, and my boss ignored my pleas. That company is still around but I was right about my part of the business. Another time, I dog-gedly insisted on pushing a new product forward until finally a sales rep asked a trusted customer to talk me out of it. I took that lesson to heart; I had become overly confident in what I wanted to achieve while the customers themselves were starting to turn away.

THERE ARE NO SILVER BULLETS. THERE ARE NO WEREWOLVES EITHER.

A common mistake made by new managers in many disciplines is an overenthusiastic focus on a new tool or methodology. As an emerging manager, it is important to discover what you can about the job ahead before you make any changes. Be careful to learn from what you are experiencing every day rather than quickly diagnosing what is wrong and becoming dogmatic about how to fix it.

For example, you may read about a practice related to measuring team compatibility or code efficiency and immediately determine that it will help you in your new assignment. It would be a mistake on several levels to immediately begin following the directions of the material you have learned. You may not understand the problem that you are solving yet, or you may not yet know what your *greatest* problem is. You may simply be too inexperienced to implement the management changes that you have read about.

All of this is not to discourage innovation or independent thinking; rather it is just encouragement to be very careful with changes when you do choose to implement them. Make sure you have thought through many different possible ramifications before you effect any management change. As in technical roles, your mind is your most important tool. Think about what you are going to do before you do it and you will be prepared for whatever comes.

Implement changes very carefully. The fact that you are in your role as the emerging manager is in itself a big change, so initially work within the processes and patterns of the person who previously held your role or within the guidelines of the company if your role is new. In other words, don't spook the team with a deluge of methodology or dogma; new managers are infamous for wanting to imprint their teams in some way. As an emerging manager, you desperately need for your team to see you as an asset that they find accessible and competent.

SHIFTING YOUR FOCUS: FROM CODE TO PEOPLE

Think about the individuals on the team and avoid thinking about yourself. The goal is to make the whole of the team achieve more than any one individual could on his or her own. How will you find the strengths of each person? How will you choose to use the strengths of each in order to build out a whole working team? Motivating each person is a different challenge altogether—once you know what you want from them, your job is to get them to do it.

Some new managers approach this problem with too radical a view, essentially pushing people to change much of their approach and routine. These new managers are excited about their own role and stay up late at night becoming giddy with visions of a Grand Unified Workplace in which everything would be perfect if they could only get everyone to do the exact right job.

The fact is that there is not a perfect environment or a perfect job, and the manager's role is sometimes to coach and sometimes to cajole behavior. If you approach the problem with big ideas but small changes, you are likely to get a better reception than with a vision that seems unreachable because of the disruption that you want to create. The term recalcitrance seems to have been created just for software engineers who adjust slowly and resist change. You can get frustrated and fight this tendency on your team, or you can leverage it.

Turn resistance into an asset that will help you temper your vision and lessen the damage of wild process or technology ideas—after all, you may be wrong sometimes. Let the viscosity of group behavior be the counterweight to your own enthusiasm. Don't be frustrated by it, but instead work on driving changes incrementally and find the limits of the organization by gauging the point at which reaction to your suggestions turns from enthusiasm to negativity.

YOUR BEST COACH MAY BE *ON* YOUR TEAM

More often than not, a development organization includes a number of great people who have been in their roles for a long time, maybe in the same company or maybe in other companies. These individuals represent a wealth of guidance for a new manager. Don't be fooled by a cold shoulder or even pedantic treatment that these senior resources sometimes apply to new managers. Often, they have either been team leads or managers themselves in the past, or they have consciously decided never to try.

The wisdom of these individuals, if they are willing to share it, can take months or years out of your own struggle to learn how to manage. Start by asking their advice, particularly on controversial issues that do not directly affect them. Ask if they have seen similar situations and how they turned out. Ask how they would take on this situation if they were in your place. Communicate your interest in their ideas and, most of all, listen. Just the fact that you asked them will create goodwill. If you listen to their answers, that's even better.

MIKE'S MANAGEMENT USE CASE

At the company where I had my first real job, there was a passionate manager who led a small group of people. Their mission was technically bleeding-edge and commercially unprecedented; the company was making a big bet on a long-shot market differentiator. If someone had given me a written description of what they were doing, I would have doubted their real prospects for success. But this manager was a passionate person with a vision, and he knew how to recruit a team.

He created an identity—the "Kong"—and used it to differentiate his team. The Kongs had desk toys and they seemed to always get mentioned at company meetings. Even though they were only eight out of eight hundred people, their status reports were blown up and posted in the hallways. It was cool to be a Kong. Kongs wanted to deliver results for their team, and they never wavered in their passion for what they were doing or their disdain for everything else. That manager captured hearts and minds; his team felt great about working very hard. The technology was dead within five years, but it would have died in five months without that manager.

In these discussions, be sure to find one or two simple things that you can latch on to as follow-up. Even if they are insignificant or irrelevant, the fact that you follow up will create a level of trust that will keep this individual coming back to your aid time and again. It can be as simple as a comment that you make in the next team meeting or an e-mail that you send with instructions on how to approach a gap in the software process.

CLOSURE

Setting goals aligns your objectives with the actions of your team. Set them well and you will have a great career as a leader, and as a manager. If you are diligent, every aspect of your work is flexible - the people, the timeline, the requirements, the equipment, etc. The leader's role is to broker an agreement that sets-up a success; the manager's role is to deliver it. Build future results while scoring short-term goals and you will be among the best at what you do.

————————

Chapter 6

PROJECTS

YOUR MANAGEMENT PROGRAM

In a technical role, you were probably used to research-ing and borrowing components or code fragments from previous projects. Most senior developers have a large library of knowledge from which to pull these shortcuts and tools, and they do not hesitate to do so as part of what is expected from their ability as top contributors.

Experience in management is no different. Managers face situations that repeat frequently just like tech-nologists do. And the best managers build tools that can readily be applied in situations that merit reuse. For managers, these tools are processes, documents, even specific expert people whom they count on. As an emerging manager, you too can start to build your tools. Generally, these take two distinct forms:

- Tools to help with ongoing operations activities— these are activities that occur periodically, regard-less of what is happening in the company. Traditional examples include status meetings, status reports, and performance reviews. You may even have these activities defined for you in your "new manager course" at work, assuming you are lucky enough to have one. Build tools to help you remember what needs to be accomplished and when. Not only will you appear organized and purposeful but you will also be using time wisely. Ongoing activities that are easy for new managers to forget include teambuilding social events, feedback sessions for your team to critique you, casual lunches with each team member, personal thanks to team members, etc. Build tools (agenda, schedule, communication format for before and after the meetings, etc.) to make all of these efforts worthwhile.

• Event-based Activities—this category refers to activities that take place when a specific event occurs. For example, many formal methodologies call for specific activities when a project is completed. You will find many other times when having a handy checklist of "what to do next" will make you do a better job and be more confident about it.

A great first tool to think about is your management program. What are your recurring meetings and when do they take place? Documenting this for your team will ensure that they can buy into your management processes and feel secure that they will meet your expectations of them. Ongoing operations activities of any sort should go on a recurring calendar that you make public. Discuss the calendar with each person and ensure that they know their role within your management program (work deadlines, administrative deadlines).

MIKE'S MANAGEMENT USE CASE

Meeting mania can take hold in any organization. That's when people spend more time in meetings than they do accomplishing real work. It is common for developers, especially the best ones, to be dragged into meetings that are ultimately frustrating to them.

I took over an organization that had meeting mania and was lucky enough to have a senior member of the team point out what was happening. Sure enough, when I asked the IT manager for records of meeting room bookings through the online reservation system, he showed me that my team spent something like 40 percent of their time in meetings. I interviewed a few random people to ask what they thought and it was unanimous: another department was disorganized and as a result my department had to communicate information to them several times, in person. The confusion of discrepancies led to more meetings and the whole cycle had been going on for three months.

Meetings do have a purpose and the communication that was happening was needed so I had to find a way to solve the problem without creating a bigger one. I decided to put out a quiet memo with just a few quick points:

1. You don't have to go to a meeting if another person from your project is already there representing you.

2. You don't have to accept any meeting that is recurring. If they want you, they can invite you every week.

3. You don't have to attend any meeting that does not have a specific agenda formalized when the meeting starts.

4. You can leave when it goes off topic or if the topics are not relevant to you.

5. You don't have to stay in any meeting more than forty-five minutes.

6. If the meeting organizer has a problem with your decision to attend, please invite me to the meeting so I can explain the policy in person.

The problem cleared up and I was an instant hero. I had never expected the sincere and complete support that I got from my team for this simple action. It was as though a weight were lifted from them immediately. And I never heard a peep from any meeting organizer.

Event-based activities are documented in simple lists that remind you about what you need to do when something happens. They are part of your management program too but not necessarily a public part. You evolve your management program over time, changing it when you learn more than you initially knew, when company policies change around you, and so on.

What Happens	Computer Program	Management Program
A new problem is provided to you.	You create a new computer program specific for that problem and save it.	You create a new management program for that situation and add it to your documentation.
You want to dry-run your solution before you use it.	Single-step debugger lets you walk through the process slowly.	You consult a more senior manager and talk about your solution.
You want your team to agree on your solution.	Code review or design review with peers. Correct mistakes pointed out in the review.	Team meeting to discuss the solution. Make concessions to get buy in.
First time to use the solution.	Triple-check everything, make a backup in case it goes badly, run.	Let impacted people know that you are using a new process. Get feedback. Act.
The solution has a problem.	Study the source code and the cause of the problem; make adjustments.	Study the cause of the problem and adapt your process. Communicate about what has changed.
The solution matures and works well.	Take out the key pieces and make them reusable for other projects.	Consider other management programs and adapt them with some of the best practices you have found. Write a book and advance the field of software development management.

Consider *defects* in software development and *mistakes* in management. If you introduced a defect in a computer program, then spent many hours resolving it, you would most likely never repeat that mistake regardless of the context of your future programs. You can do the same thing in management. If you have a management program, each time you encounter an unexpected result, you can look for ways to amend it.

Without documentation, it's as if your program were randomly choosing its own instructions. With documentation, you can take control—capturing the specific breakdown and patching it with additional management steps. Avoid being too careful and ambiguous about updates to the management program. When something goes wrong, make specific and actionable changes to the program. In this way, think of your management mistakes very positively; it is only through mistakes that your program will improve.

Below, we provide simple examples of management programs. There is no such thing as a perfect management program—they are all as different as the managers and companies that employ them. The intent of these examples is to give you a template to consider how management programs work. Look for these elements:

- Which steps are taken apparently for no specific benefit? Which later steps turn out to be possible because of this preparation?

- Which steps are necessarily sequential, i.e., would be poorly executed if done at the same time or in reverse order?

- Which steps are above and beyond vs. absolute necessities?

MANAGEMENT PROGRAM: THINGS TO DO WHEN YOU START A NEW PROJECT

- Write a clear and concise charter that has your manager's agreement. The charter should include the purpose of the work you are undertaking and the resources you will manage in doing so. A charter is not a technical document unless your customers are technical people. It should be readable in plain language that you could show anyone; in fact, everyone who is even tangentially related to the project should have a chance to read it and comment. It is a "line in the sand" that you can use to defend your decisions and recommendations later on.

- Write goals that sufficiently meet the charter. Share these with other project leaders who are dependent on you.

- Define your dependencies (things you need to get the job done—specific skills, equipment, budget, other teams' projects being on schedule, etc.) and begin working toward securing each of them. Make sure your manager knows you are dependent on these items and why.

- Define your team: people you are counting on for the new project. Unless you fully control those people's workload, make sure that you secure them for your project—possibly negotiating their allocation to your project with your boss or other managers.

Communicate this to the team, so they will understand clearly what their responsibilities are. Communicate this to your manager, so she or he will know your workload rather than overestimating your available capacity for additional work.

- Define milestones and goals. Document these in detail with your team and publish them to stakeholders. Publish a plan for how you will update everyone with information (program status meetings, status reports, demonstrations, design reviews, and so forth).

- Establish a project plan and make sure that you know how you will achieve your milestones and goals on time with the resources you have. This step will also help you identify risks and dependencies between tasks. In addition, it will give you a better understanding of dependencies on external resources, like test hardware that you may need, 3rd party software components that must be obtained or time from an expert on another team that you do not manage.

- On any larger project, maintain a risks and issues log. Use it to track a list of all *potential* risks and *real* issues that you must deal with if you are going to make the project successful. You must have a plan for every one of the items on the list including who will take the next action, and by when, so you can follow up quickly anytime you need to. Doing nothing about a risk is a perfectly valid option if you decide that the probability of the problem is too small or that the cost of counter measures would be inadequate to the scope of the problem. But you should make that decision only after careful analysis and understanding of the issue.

Without the risks and issues log, it is very easy to lose track of all the potential problems and it is nearly impossible to get to closure on them. It is extremely frustrating to see your project fail or to see your team miss a deadline because of a problem everyone anticipated but no one did anything about.

Check the log regularly, keep it updated, and hold people accountable for the actions they have committed to take (the actions they 'own' in management parlance). If you use this log as the foundation of your status updates, you will have an easy time creating very useful reports.

- Re-establish goals with each person who has been assigned to the project. They are being evaluated against new expectations, and you should make that clear. Request feedback about this change now rather than later—this will serve you well if performance problems crop up and the change is blamed.

- Check on the new project every day by discussing the status with each team member. Find a good quantitative and verifiable way to check the progress and do not rely on your or your team's subjective judgment. Ensure that the team members really have stopped work on other projects, that they really have provided transitional knowledge on old projects to other people, that the new project is advancing toward known dates at a good pace, and that there are no barriers to their success.

HONZA'S MANAGEMENT USE CASE

I am positive that almost every emerging manager (and almost every developer!) has had an experience similar to this one. After some time in my first job, I started overseeing the work of junior developers. We were working on a relatively small enhancement to an existing system and we expected it would take about three weeks to complete it.

Two weeks into the project, a developer working for me happily reported that he was almost finished; he just had some testing to do. I was happy to hear that, and I let him be.

The next week we sat down again and to my disappointment I learned that some problems were uncovered during the testing but they had nearly been overcome, and it would be done in one more week. The project slipped, but there was no real pressure on the deadline so I did not think it was a big deal.

The following week we checked the progress again, only so that I could find out that there were more problems and two components of the solution had to be completely rewritten. It was not done yet, but it should not take more than a week longer.

To make a long story short, the project took 8 weeks before the code review. After the code review was performed, it took another two weeks to clean it up and remove some glaring errors.

Obviously, the developer's inaptitude had the lion's share of responsibility for the debacle, but I also failed as a manager. There are probably a dozen lessons that can be learned from this example, but the one I want to focus on is my lack of understanding of the project's status toward completion. I never *really* knew where we were: from week two onward, there was always just a week of work left, but that week took two months! I relied on a subjective estimate of the remaining work, but I never really knew whether the work that was supposedly complete was really done!

Avoid this error if you can and always track metrics or interim milestones which are as objective as possible. Depending on the type of work or project, you may want to measure the number of implemented and tested use cases or function points. You may set interim milestones by which an increment of functionality is expected to be fully implemented, tested and demonstrable to the stakeholders. Later in the project or product lifecycle, you may want to measure the number of outstanding defects or open support cases. You will see that your team will be grateful and more confident because they will know exactly where they are in the project, and you will have real data that you can show to management and customers with confidence.

MANAGEMENT PROGRAM: WHEN YOU
TAKE ON AN EXISTING PROJECT

- Determine who the customer is and what he or she expects from the product. A customer is someone who is willing to give up his or her resources in exchange for your product. Test this carefully to make sure you know exactly what your goals should be (versus the ones that were handed down to you as a "given" that may be ill founded). Don't underestimate the power of re-examining the specifics of who are customers and what they have purchased; from the commercial perspective, that's all that matters.

- Establish existing commitment specifics, schedules, and current perceptions of what is happening with the project. Again, don't assume that you are being provided with the full set of information needed to take over management. Determine these things for yourself in order to build your own conviction about what must be done, and possibly in order to discover opportunity for changes in scope, resources, or timing that your predecessor may have overlooked. After all, the reason you were put in charge must be some sort of problem with the previous manager.

- Just like on a new project, reestablish the project plan as well as the risks and issues log. If there was no concrete document of risks and issues before you took over, take time now to create it before you agree to lead the project. Certainly you will want a reliable project plan in place before you commit a date. These documents are tools that provide a very effective way to truly understand the project. Without them you will not know the most important actions that must be taken to get or keep the project on track.

- Determine who is on the team and their level of commitment, their caliber, and their actual level of expertise. Never rely on any factor other than tangible capability that you can validate.

- Determine who is motivated and who is not, what their motivations are, and especially what their expectations are. Find out about any interpersonal issues, within or outside the department. Again, observe for yourself what is happening instead of trusting information handed to you.

Complete your own management program with whatever level of detail you need. Some managers will more intuitively handle the transition from technical to managerial and may need only a few reminders of specific administrative activities. Others will struggle more with the transition and may document dozens of processes. Your management program is personal and customized by you.

MIKE'S MANAGEMENT USE CASE

I've evolved a simple project plan format that I like a lot for small teams. Basically, I start with a list of people, a list of tasks, and a time frame for completion. A matrix with the names down one side and weeks across the top defines a calendar.

In a team meeting, we fill in the calendar with assignments that each person wants to tackle.

Everyone buys into their assignment and the projected time that will be required to complete it.

Each person has a row on the calendar and each column represents a week of time. Inside each cell, a task such as "Module X Code Start" or "Module X code progress 40 percent" shows the goals of each person for the week. During weekly team meetings, we review the progress to date and either check off the completed work or change the matrix with everyone's agreement.

The schedule is posted very publicly, and team members work very hard to be able to check off their square each week. Often, when a team member has not completed the work, he or she chooses to leave the matrix unchanged and commits to double up for two check marks the following week. People want to be successful; they don't want to disappoint their peers, and they want to complete. If you create a simple environment that aligns those human characteristics of individuals with the productivity goals of the company, you will be a better manager than most.

PROJECT PLAN

Managers are often ridiculed as mouse-pushing obsessive maintainers of detailed and absurdly unrealistic project plans. Disconnected from reality, these caricatures are usually bizarre figures that spend their days carefully documenting whether resource X spent three-point-two hours on task A, and then went for lunch, or whether the uncanny dependency on task C made resource X sit idle in her cubicle the whole morning. Nothing could be further from the truth in the case of a good project manager.

What a UML model is for an architect, a project plan is for the project manager. It is a blueprint of the program, a map showing a path to success as well as areas inhabited by lions and dragons. A good project plan, particularly in software development, does not try to capture every detail and minute nuance of the project. Rather, it identifies the main tasks and critical dependencies, sketching a viable approach to the finish line.

Think of a project plan as a simulation. It is a model which helps validate or disprove the hypothesis that the project can be completed as planned. It is a tool which, if used consistently and systematically, can help you avoid basic mistakes such as overloading people with two tasks at a time or forgetting about the vacation-laden summer months.

Most importantly, the project plan is not static. In software development, an industry full of surprises and unanticipated obstacles, the project plan must be a living document that undergoes constant change. Always reflecting the best available information at that moment, the current state of the project should match the state that the plan reflects for today's date. The project plan should not include any people doing work unless they are truly committed to the effort. The amount of time projected by the QA team to properly complete QA should be on the plan.

Keeping the plan up to date is a fine art and you will only learn to do it well over time. If you put too much detail in the plan, you will either spend excessive time updating it, or you will abandon it when it becomes hopelessly neglected. On the other hand, if you do not include enough detail, you will not have confidence in the projections it provides.

Even the best project plan is no good unless it is executed well. Do not get comfortable when you have created the perfect project plan. This is not the time to head to Hawaii (unless you work there)—the hard work is only starting! The plan will not run the project for you. It will only tell you the best currently known path to project completion, and where you currently stand relative to that ideal path. Your everyday job is to identify obstacles on the path and keep your team on task.

As soon as you see that you might be getting off track, you must take actions to get things back under control. What actions you take, how creative, effective and innovative you are, defines your skill as the project manager. In this light, project management is suddenly not the most boring and mundane chore on earth. It can be a creative and intellectually challenging job which requires an inquisitive and bright mind.

HONZA'S MANAGEMENT USE CASE

I had a chance to work with an emerging manager who was resisting the idea of putting a project plan in place. His excuses were that the project had too many unknowns and that any project plan would become invalid a day after it was created. Even though I passionately disagreed, I was not able to persuade him. In the end, I let him try to run the project his way—it was his project after all and the consequences of a potential delay were relatively mild. It seemed like an ideal project to help the emerging manager learn a lesson.

Three weeks into the project, the manager realized that he could not make any decisions. Without a plan to contrast against the current status, he did not know whether he was on track to deliver the project or not. He still had six weeks left until the deadline but he did not know whether he was running ahead or behind the schedule. He could not tell whether he needed more people, a lesser scope, or whether he had enough time to squeeze in some overdue legacy code refactoring.

When the team ran into a problem and offered the manager two alternative solutions, he had nothing to go on but instinct. He could only watch from the sidelines as his people stumbled to completion four weeks late.

The lesson here is not that the project was late because there was no project plan. In fact, the project may have been late even with a project plan. The lesson is that the lack of a project plan reduced the *manager* to the role of an *observer*. He had to operate in a void, with no model of expected events to compare with actual ones. His actions must have lacked confidence that was sorely needed.

When creating the project plan, do not assume that it is a solitary activity that must be performed in the seclusion of your corner office. In fact, we have found it very useful to make a habit of getting the team involved in the creation and finalization of project plans. Even if the team is not interested in the whole process, or if it is not practical to involve everyone, make sure you at least review the final draft with as many team members as reasonable. You will often find yourself making substantial changes based their feedback. The resulting project plan will be better than one created without the team, and most importantly you will get much more buy-in if the key team members feel responsible for it.

HONZA'S MANAGEMENT USE CASE

I was leading a small team of engineers on a relatively innovative project. The plan called for a series of medium-sized releases of new functionality but it was plagued by problems from the outset. The application platform which we assumed would be rock solid turned out to be full of defects and large portions had to be rewritten to work for our purposes. Even worse, as one thing turned out wrong after another, I realized that I was the only person who felt responsible for meeting the deadlines. Working late nights and weekends, I was alone trying to save the project.

First I blamed my team for having no drive and for being irresponsible. But then I realized that I was the source of the problem. I estimated the whole project. I put the project plan together. I acted as if the project was personally mine, not the team's.

I learned a very valuable lesson. With the next release of the product, I was very careful to get the team involved in the estimation process. I had them review the project plan and affirm their commitment to the scope and milestones that we set.

None of the subsequent releases were easy, but we never missed a deadline after that. We always started with a better project plan because the team kept me honest and did not allow me to underestimate the effort or subscribe to unrealistic goals. And because I obtained everyone's buy-in, I could hold them accountable.

Inevitably, every emerging manager faces the question of what tool to use for project plan documents. Your company may already have a PMO (Project Management Office) which defines best practices in project management, including which tools and templates should be used. Some clients, such as governments and global multi-nationals may even require that you use specific tools so they can audit your plans or easily merge them with plans from other companies. If you are not working in an environment that prescribes project management tools and methods, consult an experienced colleague.

Microsoft® Project is the default answer for many managers. It is very powerful software but it can be challenging to learn to use well. Used poorly, it is extremely frustrating and time consuming. Consider the size of the project you have to manage and how much time you can spend on project management. Especially on your first project as a leader, you will have so many things to worry about that learning a new tool can push you right over the edge! When you decide that you want to make an investment in learning a project management tool, we recommend that you spend some quality time with a book and in a short training course. You will gain confidence with any tool much faster if you get some help and there is no point in hacking your way through without training.

You can always just maintain your plan in a spreadsheet, without the need for specialized tools. Typically, you would have the timeline across the top (days, weeks or months) and rows representing people. You can do it the other way around too; it just depends on whether you have a longer time with fewer people or vice-versa. Each cell indicates what a person is supposed to be doing at any given time, which is exactly what you need when you are checking up on things.

Especially for new managers, this approach can be much more intuitive and productive than learning a new specialized tool.

Some managers decide not to use software tools to manage project plans at all. A fun and very approachable way is to organize project tasks on a whiteboard or on a wall, using magnets or sticky notes. This is very practical for smaller co-located teams: Everyone can see the plan all the time, which facilitates discussion, adjustments and accountability.

HONZA'S MANAGEMENT USE CASE

An emerging manager that was working with me found himself frustrated by the strict software development methodology that was in use at our company. He was considering an alternative methodology for use on one of his pet projects that was about to start. Excited by the many simple yet smart ideas found in the modern agile development methodology, he decided to give it a try. Unfortunately, he misunderstood what he read and got a bit too radical with his approach. In his interpretation, Agile meant no management whatsoever, and most importantly, no project plan. He just set a relatively vague goal and said "go!" Everyone on the team got busy and started working on *stuff*.

After a month of meandering, they had to acknowledge that they were not any closer to the goal than they were when they started. Sure, they had developed some cool platform components, but they did not really provide any useful functionality. Much more work on the platform was still needed before anything useful could be built.

Two months into the project, the situation was very similar. The platform components were even cooler, but there were no tangible benefits from the work done.

The problem was a lack of project planning. Don't cringe at this analysis just because your past experience tells you that a project plan is an incomprehensible document that gets stashed away in the manager's private folders. It can just as well be a set of sticky notes glued on a whiteboard. It does not have to be a complex model predicting the future of our planet and everything else. A list of the most noteworthy goals that must be achieved during the next two weeks will do. The point is to always know whether the project remains on track, or is lost in the woods. No matter what form it takes, it is still a plan. Without a plan, you are not applying agile development or any other methodology; you are living in sheer anarchy.

THE UNIVERSAL MANAGEMENT LANGUAGE OF MEASUREMENT

While software development is a creative skill in many ways, there is a quantitative backbone to any project, and you should work to understand it well. There are countable *features*, *hours worked*, and *costs* at a raw level. There are function points, lines of code, defects, test cases, and other units of work at a higher level. It is important that as a manager, you learn to ask for these figures, study them, and find the patterns in their change. In every department that you will ever manage, you will always encounter measurements that can guide you toward success.

This idea could be very new to you. In the past, you may have felt that measurements and the tools that collected them were a colossal waste of time. After all, measurements provide ridiculously detailed information like "Today, quality is at 78.6 percent." You were right to consider such facts as irrelevant to yourself when you were an individual contributor. But once you are responsible for many more people than just yourself, it is precisely these values that will change over time and paint a performance landscape that you would otherwise not see. That perspective will help you with all of these points:

- To separate emotion from fact. Your team may be under-producing, or it may be overloaded. But without facts, you may not know the difference.

- To empower your management actions. If you provide facts about your team's performance and workload, you are more likely to achieve agreement from upper management about adding resources, changing dates, and other important requests.

- To simplify your decision process. As an individual contributor, you worked with your own skills and time, continuously evaluating every action and choosing a next step. Once you are managing a broader and broader team, you will lack that clear understanding of what everyone is achieving as a whole at any given time.

You won't find your management job automated by any of the benefits on that list. Measurements don't replace the need for judgment and person-to-person interaction any more than a car speedometer replaces the need for a driver. But they do provide a second opinion, an oracle of information, if you know how to interpret their values.

If you are fortunate, your company will have provided accurate tools and ways to measure activities that you manage. In many cases, the tools are absent or they are overly complicated and fundamentally not useful. Regardless of what you are obligated to do, you can put valuable metrics to work for you if you master some basics.

METRIC BASICS

You can find facts about anything that you want to include in your measurement process. The key is to follow a few rules:

- If the facts are not being collected, establish a process to gather them and appoint an owner who will be responsible for following that process. Avoid labor-intensive measurements as these will introduce new costs and error.

- Ensure that you have several months of historical facts before you start using them to make decisions.

In some cases, you can calculate measurements for historical periods from archived data.

- Remove any arbitrary component that is involved in collecting the facts.

It may be necessary to join several interrelated facts in order to produce a single metric value that provides insightful information. Classic metric readings include things like "lines of code per developer per year" or "cost per developer hour." These calculations provide an easy way to get a handle on important values that may follow real-world results more closely than any isolated number.

Another important consideration is the scope of a measurement. Some things have meaningful quasi-instantaneous values, such as the number of defects that are being found each day. Others require a cumulative calculation over a period of time, such as a comparison of total hours worked to total hours estimated for a project.

TRENDS AND RANGES

A common mistake is to take a single metric reading in isolation and react to it; the fact is that metric readings are pointless without context, including historical values for comparison. The change in a metric reading that covers the same calculation over a period of time is called a *trend*. Trends are useful as a means of enlightening you about the impact of real-world changes that you have decided to implement. Look for the trend of a metric to change when you implement a management policy. Decide for yourself whether the metric is going in the right direction based on what you have changed.

Similarly, ranges are a useful way of looking at metrics. A stoplight analogy is an example of a metric *range* tool. It is not useful to look at all of the digits of precision of a metric because metrics are changed by many underlying factors. But it may be useful to call the metric "red, yellow, or green" when the measurement reaches certain values for more than five days, weeks, etc. The key to using ranges is that you can determine *in advance* what values you expect to experience in any one metric. You might not take notice of a metric that is slowly climbing, but if you established that the metric should never go past a certain point, then you can check yourself and your management policy when it does. The metric spreadsheet turns "red" and signals an alarm—something in those fundamental facts is out of whack and you're in charge of the fix.

As a technologist, you might object to the notion of a stoplight or other metric trending tool. After all, saying that a project is 'red' or 'green' provides almost no actionable information because the facts are all but lost. What it does provide, however, is a way to incorporate your status with that of other managers in a roll-up report of a broader organization. Such a report is likely to be the only useful input for a senior manager that oversees a large area of the business. For that manager, and for you, trend reports serve to direct *attention*. Green means 'move on to the next report' while 'red' means 'stop and dig in to the facts.'

MANAGING BY THE NUMBERS

Metrics are the gauges in your management cockpit. For example, take your project plan and check the actual rate of new defect creation against your estimated time to complete QA. If the trend of new defects is not declining, your plan should not show that QA is near complete. You can envision many different meaningful comparisons when you think of the project plan as a map of what is ahead, and the metrics as a visual check on your current position.

When it is time to take management action, consider in advance how you expect to influence your metrics. For example, if you are considering a methodology change that will improve your developers' efficiency, which metrics will show the actual improvement? Armed with before and after metric values, you can assess for yourself whether you had the intended effect, or not. If it worked, you can be certain of your next step along similar lines; if it did not, you may consider reversing the action or taking a different tack. Either way, you learned a lot more than you would have without a metric.

Methodologies for metrics and how to manage with them vary widely. While you can find expert guidance elsewhere on this topic, some consistently important points are:

- Your people will align *easily* to measurements. When technical team members understand what is being measured, they will respond with behaviors that impact the measurement. While potentially disastrous (if you count lines of code as a measure of productivity, the developers will start writing drawn out code), you can use this fact to your advantage. Simply align your goals with the things you are measuring, which is a sensible thing to do anyway. Associate rewards (individual recognition, bonuses, special events) with successes that are being measured to guarantee both success and consistency in your management.

Spend extra time defining the right quantitative measures that support your goals and minimize negative or unintended side effects. Sometimes you may need to put two or more measures in place, so they can check and balance each other. Achieving a coding deadline is pointless without a quality check. A great product that is three times over budget deserves a second look.

- Estimates are metrics too. Measurements that contrast estimated duration with actual duration for any given piece of work are valuable as a means of evaluating individual contribution. Don't be afraid to use estimates as factual inputs to your measurement process as long as you consistently use the same experts to provide the estimates.

- Defects can be scheduled. While it is true that any single defect can be incredibly difficult to resolve, it is also true that defects, in aggregate, can be classified and scheduled. Projects can seem to be on track for 80 percent of the scheduled time only to suddenly freeze as the team enters chaos on a defect resolution treadmill. This can happen because of poor coding or design, but it can also happen because you are not managing the defect resolution process to a schedule. The solution is to track defect trends and take management actions aimed at supporting your quality, timeline or functionality goals.

CLOSURE

Make your own management program that reminds you of the things you need to do when you think it is important to be consistent. Be sure to include soft things like personal thanks, public celebrations and awards within those process steps because they are a very real part of how you reward your team. Change the program with every experience to make it perform better just like you do when you are testing new software.

Write a project plan to help you predict what is going to happen based on current circumstances and a reasonable expectation for progress. Initiate management actions that align the predicted outcome of the plan to the goals that you are trying to achieve. Every aspect of your project should be in play if your plan predicts failure. The people that follow you are counting on the fact that your direction will make them successful.

Finally, use measurements to get objective validation for your management actions and for your project plan.

———————

Chapter 7

PEOPLE

This chapter is about the most important asset you will manage: the team and the people on it. People may seem like a very simple topic—we meet them every day, we talk to them, spend vacations with them, go to lunch with them. There is nothing mysterious or magical about interacting with people. (Yes, there are exceptions!) In fact, interacting with people in the work environment should be even simpler because there are always well-defined topics to discuss, clear tasks to give and clear objectives, which can be easily controlled.

And yet, a manager's hands-on job for the bulk of each day is to work with people. As it turns out, working with people is difficult and demanding, but also rewarding. People will make you live through some of the most miserable moments of your career but also through some of the most exhilarating moments of your life. This section should help you make sure that there will be more of the latter.

As an emerging manager, especially one with a deeply technical background (as opposed to a manager with a "soft" background, e.g., from sales or consulting, etc.), you may tend to underestimate the "people" factor.

Being focused on the "hard" problems, such as schedules, design hurdles, deliverables, plans, code, and thousands of other things, you may ignore and overlook the human factor:

- What motivates each person?

- What is the value system of each person?

- What is the background and skill set of each person?

- What are each individual's personal problems and how are their moods affected?

- What makes each person happy? Annoyed?

These are the little differences and imperfections that make each person unique. Don't treat them like machines, with exact and precise communications that are stone cold and impersonal. You may be consistent and fair in your own view, yet blind to the unique perspective of the person you are trying to motivate. Don't expect mechanistic and clear responses from your team; the impact of things you do will not be immediately obvious. As notoriously bad communicators, software developers often do not send clear signals about things they like or dislike. If you push someone too far, too fast, he or she may break down and stop respecting you. Once that happens, the damage is done; there's no simple "undo" in management. Communicate slowly, with repeated messages, and follow up in person when the slightest concern is raised.

MIKE'S MANAGEMENT USE CASE

Outstanding people on your team will get you outstanding results. Certainly management is about dealing with everyone, not just the best or the worst, but by the same token your goal is to improve the average with every move you make. Outstanding people are to be found everywhere around you—at work and elsewhere. Anyone you notice, from eavesdropping at a coffee house to visiting the accounting department, can be an asset on your team. Make a habit of introducing yourself to people who impress you, anywhere, and let them know what you do, how you think about building careers. These people may want to work for you and, if there is a way for them to do so, they will be willing followers because of your early attention to their strengths.

Be honest with yourself and unless you have a reason to believe that you are a naturally great people manager and that your people skills at least match if not surpass your technical skills (which is a rare phenomenon in software development), please view this chapter for the importance it really has. We will try to point out some problematic areas that you should be aware of, help you see pitfalls that you would not otherwise dodge easily, and preview unfamiliar but quite typical situations that you will soon encounter.

Most people are not *born* great people managers, and some will never reach that state. But most of us can get *better* at managing people, and even small steps can take you a long distance.

LEADERS AND MANAGERS

There are two roles you will play on a daily basis when managing the team: the role of a leader and that of a manager. Each is different and success in your new role requires both.

The leader provides an essential vision and inspiration that motivates and builds willpower in the team. The leader has an idea of what should be achieved and can share it with eloquence, even if in a style that is unique. Leaders are passionate, determined, and confident. They can get others excited and can create common goals for unity of effort. Leaders do not waver before obstacles but instead they charge directly toward them. All of this happens by influence and example. Followers are attracted to the role model of their leader.

Managers, on the other hand, have a much more tangible, frontline role. The manager addresses people individually and fits the work and workplace to their needs. The manager works on behalf of the team to improve chances for success. The manager is less glamorous but more specific and immediate than the leader. But if the manager can at the same time be a leader, that's the best of all.

MIKE'S MANAGEMENT USE CASE

One of my first leaders was also one of my best. During college, I worked a manufacturing job and applied for a part-time programming role in the IT department at the same company. I was offered the programming assignment a few months later, and I was excited until I found out they were not going to give me a raise. I contacted the human resources department, and they explained that because I was already an employee I could not be paid more, even in a different job. Of course, they knew I wanted the programming job, and they knew I was willing to work for manufacturing wages, so they were just trying to save a few dollars by "lowballing" me. So I contacted my foreman on the manufacturing floor to make sure he still needed me, and when he said yes, I turned *down* the programming job.

I wish I could have been a fly on the wall when the IT leader heard what human resources had done to me! Within thirty minutes, a recruiter contacted me urgently, called me Sir, and offered a 70 percent raise to "please" take the programming role!

Like any great manager, my new boss in the IT department chose me because he knew I would add value to his department. He understood that the meager savings that might have come from paying me "just enough" would be far offset by my disillusionment with the role. He knew the HR rules, and just how far they would bend.

I took the job because he stood up for me. He became a mentor that I could trust, and I produced results for him that were far beyond his expectations.

THE LEADER ROLE

Some people seem to be "born leaders," but others learn how to do it, so you are covered either way. In fact, because you decided to step up and manage a team, you have already demonstrated the spirit of leadership, if only for your own career. A great place to start understanding leadership better is to consider how leaders are different from other team members in practical, visible ways. Leaders, for example, seem to understand how the effort of the team results in *financial* benefits for the company. You may think this is trivial—if so, you are probably approaching the question too simplistically. What are all the costs of having the team in place and what is all the value of the work product that is created? Why is the work product useful and to whom, and why do they want to buy it instead of making it themselves? Are your profits sustainable because your clients profit when they do business with you? Or do clients view your products as a necessity for now, that will eventually become obsolete?

Seemingly philosophical, these questions are actually important because they allow the leader to *remove* goals or efforts that are not *essential* to the outcome. The leader understands how the product is used. She or he understands why it is successful, especially when compared to competitors' products. The leader often knows and communicates with end customers. She or he thinks about anything that might harm the product or team. The leader is enthusiastic about the product and about *change*. She or he understands all dependencies and engages with other teams to ensure that

146

everything is going smoothly. Always looking for opportunity, the leader's arsenal includes persuasion with which to seize it.

But the leader is not a know-it-all. Believe it or not, the job boils down to *listening and thinking*. Think about your own experiences with people whom you consider great leaders. Oftentimes, it is the people who ask the hardest, simplest questions that we respect the most. Leaders do not accept what they are told but rather they verify facts and use their experience to make novel observations.

THE MANAGER ROLE

A manager's responsibility is to keep things going and to make sure that results are achieved in a timely and predictable manner. Many great managers are also wonderful leaders, and some are also excellent technical experts in their area, but it is important to realize that management is a distinct role.

Managers direct all or part of an organization or business toward its goals by guiding the use of resources: human, financial, material, etc. Management roles come in many flavors. Our focus here is on one specific facet of how you will emerge as a leader in software development: managing people. In the software industry, people are typically a company's major asset, and highest expense.

Management means achieving results through people. If that's not your goal, stop right here. As a manager, you will not produce anything. The entire management structure exists to create and foster the activities of the people who actually do something.

Managing confident, independent, extremely well-educated and smart software developers in the twenty-first century is a brand-new field of skill. Cultural mélange, technical task complexity, growing problem scope, and novel methodologies all overlap in the development manager's in-box. An early lesson that many great managers have learned is that the working environment needs to be democratic. This tends to produce better results than a rigid command hierarchy. For a number of reasons, it works best for organizations with strong intellect and talent.

The manager's role in this environment is not to issue commands, but to *serve* the team. This is another good stopping point if that's not what you intend to do with your time! By making sure that each team member's needs are met, and that there are no obstacles impeding their progress, the manager moves the project forward. Don't take this to extremes, of course, service here means tending to professional needs. But the manager's job does include an astonishingly wide range of activities:

- Providing a steady stream of well-formulated tasks, suitable to the skills and experience level of the recipients and prioritized by the business

- Making decisions of any nature that result in a better operation for the team

- Ensuring that everyone has access to the right information and that the right communication channels exist

- Shielding the team from external interference but also exposing them to the business if it adds value, or if it helps them understand the importance of what they are doing

- Improving lives of the team members in any way that is reasonable, within the cost/benefit constraints of budget and company policy.

- Enforcing processes

- Shaping and structuring the team, so it runs efficiently and becomes less dependent on the manager

- Monitoring productivity of the team and identifying performance problems

- Motivating the team

- Providing feedback and helping the team grow as individuals and as a group

- Getting individuals to produce their highest level of quality—to be the best they can—in the process of achieving a goal that is reasonable and necessary

In short, the leader may provide initial motivation, but the manager creates opportunity and coaches the best performance from every team member. The manager sets the scene and lets the team perform. The team manager is an organizer, judge, psychologist, accountant, negotiator, mentor, coach, leader, as well as patient listener.

THE ORGANIZATION CHART IS UPSIDE DOWN

With all of these hats to wear, the manager is usually the one who is also held responsible for success or failure of the team. This burden of responsibility comes with higher authority and power, which is why the traditional organization chart shows fewer and fewer people as you go "up" the management chain. But the reality is that all of that power as it concentrates upward exists to prepare and set up each successive level below to do their best and deliver results. As an individual contributor in some part of the software engineering function, you probably never thought of management as a service to you. But that's precisely how you should think of it when you emerge as a new manager.

MIKE'S MANAGEMENT USE CASE

Three times over the years, I have identified complicated management situations that required the same specific technique. In each case, I was working with very talented people who felt they were not being recognized and rewarded appropriately. These individuals worked very hard and were considered valuable. But in each case, they were disappointed with career progress and were in the late stages of leaving my company.

They were special because for all of them, success was limited by actions or patterns in their professional behavior that were not directly related to their tremendous contribution. For example, one of them had a tendency to send out abusive communications and showed uncooperative demeanor at an extreme level.

At first, I provided simple feedback: get in a conference room, outline the problem, and write it all down for the next formal performance review. But the patterns continued, even as their competency and contribution to the business in creased.

A second round of feedback revealed that these individuals felt that the very thing I was criticizing was precisely what made them successful. For example, direct communications, which others found abusive, resulted in very efficient dialogue! It seemed I could not address the problem without hurting their performance.

In each case, I decided to take it slow and be consistent. I spoke very often with these individuals—almost immediately after even the slightest suspect behavior. We talked about alternative approaches, and I proposed crutches and shortcuts so they could remember how to avoid the patterns. Two out of three worked after about six weeks of attention.

Management empowerment as "the boss" is essential for success, but not in the traditional sense. Your management authority should help you play a special role *within* the team, without placing yourself *above* the team.

No level of authority is going to make people on the team respect you, and respect is what you need if you are going to persuade and motivate. Build a relationship of mutual respect with the team members by helping them rather than competing against them. For example, avoid taking credit for achievements; your leaders know your role in the work of everyone on your team, so you don't need to remind anyone of who is in charge. On every possible occasion, deflect the praise to you onto the team and its individual members, but do so sincerely.

Always work for your team. Give them privileges first, waiting to get your own privileges from your manager. Get your team members what they want when you can and when it is justified. Your rewards come later when leadership extends and becomes the dominant dimension of your compensation.

A SERVANT TO THE TEAM

As you get more and more accustomed to the idea that you are there for your team, not vice versa, you will start realizing that this is a very difficult role. There will be so many things you could do for your team. Rather, there will be so many things that you *should* do for your team! But you will not be able to fulfill every wish. You will realize that some demands are unreasonable and irrelevant for success. You will look at all possible improvements that you could put into practice and you will realize that they each have a different priority, and they each offer a different return. Great! That means that you are thinking about your job.

Your role is to achieve the maximum efficiency of your team by removing obstacles and equipping them with the right tools. You must make them feel good about their jobs by providing rewards, recognition and worthy goals. But that does not mean fulfilling every whimsical wish and it does not mean spending money without proper justification. Showering the team with expensive yet ineffective equipment, training or parties may look great for a while but the team will soon realize that you are not acting smart and the effect will be short lived. After all, the money that you have been throwing out the window could have been just as well applied to their paychecks!

Spend corporate budget money and other resources on your team like you would spend your **own** money and time on a good friend or family member. You want everything for them, but you cannot live beyond your means or those of your role. You need to understand the importance of each decision you make. Compare the specific cost in terms of money and time against the return that you expect, keeping in mind that the return may be soft and intangible, such as increased loyalty or higher motivation. Ultimately, you want to feel that you applied your available resources in the best possible way for the benefit of the team and company.

HONZA'S MANAGEMENT USE CASE

Software development is a rapidly evolving field, so you will find that most good developers are hungry for additional education and eager to build new skills. Training is a great example of an area where you can either spend a lot of money with very limited effect, or very little money with a huge impact. Purchasing external training is an obvious (and expensive) option. You may find that what people really want is a professional certification, so you can sponsor their growth by providing study time at work or by paying the certification exam fees. Organized in-house study groups are another inexpensive yet effective tool.

I was once at a company that never invested any training time or money in my growth. I raised this issue with my manager and after some discussion he agreed to send me for a rather expensive external training. When he finally approved the training, I was happy and felt valued—I sure must have been worth something to the company if they did this for me!

But when the week of the training finally came, I was disappointed. The instructor did not really know any thing about the subject that I had not discovered by myself. He was not able to answer the hard questions that challenged me. During the week, I learned one or two things but definitely not enough to justify the cost. I still appreciated that my manager sponsored my education, but the *value* of this investment diminished suddenly in my eyes.

That outcome is not as unusual as you might think. Especially for the brightest developers, it is extremely challenging to identify appropriate instructors and in-depth training programs. Another problem is that if people do not use newly acquired skills immediately, they are often forgotten so your well-meant cost and effort goes to waste. You will also find that the people who complained the most about the lack of training will be the first and loudest critics of training done wrong.

External training is still valuable for topics where you do not have enough in-house expertise, or if you know that the training program is proven and will meet your needs. But for training, just like for other areas, there is an art to spending your budget effectively.

IF YOU LOVE SOMETHING...

As the manager, your goal is to build a healthy and self-confident team that is capable of more, bigger things over time. You need to be able to leave the team (on vacation, when you are promoted, etc.) without it falling apart. Nothing exemplifies the transition from engineer/developer into management as well as the apparent contradiction that is implied by that statement.

As an engineer, you were more valuable when you were doing more things yourself, directly impacting the production of your group. In fact, the most admirable direct contributors are usually the workhorses—those who are obviously on the job and focused on useful work most of the time. Managers, on the other hand, are least valuable when output is directly dependent on them. If things grind to a halt when the manager is not present, that is a sign of a team that is too dependent, or a manager who is too controlling. Managers who can apparently always take time out to talk to people, who seem to get the job done easily and can even go on vacation at a moment's notice are admired by their peers. These managers work hard on things that are *important*, because the things that are *urgent* have all been delegated.

SO MUCH TO LEARN

By now you are hopefully starting to understand the full picture of the complexity of management. It is not an easy thing to do well, and you can make it happen only by careful delegation of bigger responsibilities to the team members, by constant coaching and consulting, by developing yourself and your team. You have to perform many functions that have nothing to do with immediate output on your current project, which is counterintuitive to your engineering/development roots. Your efforts will be far less than perfect, and you will know it right away even when you don't know why. You can easily get frustrated thinking that you *should* do more than you *can* do.

Do not despair. Every great manager experiences this same dilemma. Experience will make you a better manager, just the same way that experience improved your abilities as an individual contributor. As an engineer, your mistakes did not impact other people and could often be overcome before anyone knew about them. Do not be discouraged by the fact that management mistakes are irrevocably public. As long as you stay focused on improving, and you work diligently toward being a better manager, every mistake can be overcome.

Approach it like any other challenge. Read, take advice from others if you can. Observe people who appear to be good leaders and managers and learn from them. Experiment and use what has worked before but always be ready for surprise. There are over six billion people inhabiting this small planet and each of them is different. Each team is different too and has a different spirit. More experience will make you better prepared, but you will never fully solve this puzzle.

KEEPING IN TOUCH WITH THE TEAM

Recall your own days as an expert software engineer. You or at least many of the people you worked with were not the most communicative examples of *Homo sapiens*. New problems were typically digested and analyzed "solo" before escalating to someone else. In short, your manager probably spent a lot of time wondering what you were doing and even more time frustrated that you did not ask for more help. As an emerging manager, you won't make that same mistake with your team. You will stay tuned-in to their efforts and celebrate new problems by getting everyone's opinion. You will condition your team to expect to see you often and to get great results from their interactions with you because you follow up and make things happen for them.

Everyone on the team should know they can come to you at any time to discuss any problem. Don't hide in a big office, even if they offer you one, since that's a sure-fire way to separate yourself and ensure nobody tells you anything. In fact, move as close to the team as possible. Try to always have a complete picture of what the team is doing and what are the hot problems of the day.

This may not be an issue for you if you manage a small team, let's say between two and four people, and you all work together all the time. But as soon as the team grows, it becomes difficult to keep in touch with everyone. Even in small teams, there is a real risk of you getting so overloaded with project related problems and everyday issues that you lose contact with the people when it comes to the main thing they need for you to care about: themselves. If you don't seem to care about your people, they will lack motivation, fail to perform, or even leave. Carve out some of your time to meet with everyone and get to know them.

TEAM MEETINGS

You will want to meet with the team in a group and with your direct reports one-on-one weekly. Hold these meetings in addition to the ongoing issue driven discussions and project status meetings. Even if you feel like you are in touch with the team constantly, resist the temptation to skip team meetings and one-on-ones. Instead, use this time to step away from the day-to-day activities. During this time, you can:

- Discuss and plan future training programs, either from team member to team member or externally.

- Get ideas from team members about how to improve your team in other ways—tools, outings, etc.

- Find out about other teams and people outside of your own scope.

- Tell your team about the company, the market, or competitors so they understand the broader effort.

- Identify team members who might, like you, be emerging managers.

- Engage your team in activities outside of the department, like recruiting, social or activity committees, etc.

All of these activities center on aligning your team to broader objectives: growth, improvement, communication, etc. None of these objectives are relevant in program status meetings about defects and code completion dates, versions, etc. If you don't create a venue for this sort of discussion, it will not happen on its own. While projects will still be completed, the environment in which your people operate will be far inferior to the experience you could provide otherwise.

The team meeting's primary purpose is to allow everyone to catch up with everyone else and identify common problems. A secondary purpose is always to introduce whatever changes are coming, with a lot of context about why change is occurring. Team meetings are not specifically oriented at solving anything; progress does not have to be tracked or discussed in this forum. Rather, what you want to do is give everyone a chance to present highlights of their recent work that may be especially interesting to others or relevant to the whole group. Common problems, needs, or complaints can be discussed openly, along with suggestions for ways to improve. New ideas or "vision" for the product may be brought up and discussed. Relations among team members are built and strengthened.

This time is also a perfect chance to update the team on activities elsewhere in the company (make sure you are informed—it is an important part of being a leader), present and explain new policies or announce upcoming events. Do not hesitate to invite guests occasionally if there is a relevant topic that they could help discuss or explain, but keep it relevant.

HOW TO RUN A TEAM MEETING

In a group setting, balance between talking and listening is important. You have to share important or interesting information with your team, but you will get the most value for yourself when you listen to everyone else. Make everyone get involved. Ask the quiet people explicitly for their opinion, and silence the chatterboxes overtly so they don't waste everyone's time. (Don't worry, if they really are over talkers, they will be used to being told to be quiet!) Sometimes, you can ask someone to prepare material that he or she will share with the team;

other times, go around the table and let everyone talk for a few minutes about achievements and problems.

Don't monopolize the discussion in team meetings. Pause at moments where you expect that the attendees might want to extend or oppose your message. Support anyone who is speaking by maintaining eye contact and signal that you are listening carefully (nodding, taking notes, etc.). Ask open-ended questions and expect long answers that require several people to elaborate. An example of an open-ended question is "What could we do with this problem?" An example of a closed question, on the other hand, is "Can we do something with this problem?" Obviously, the first version of the question opens gates of creativity and forces people to think about options, while the latter offers an easy escape in the answer NO.

Like any meeting, team gatherings require an agenda. A list on a whiteboard will suffice but bring a prepared list if you have especially long topics to cover. Team members should have the right to add items to the agenda and set the priorities for the meeting time. It's not a coffee break or a sports update; informal banter is a good idea if it helps to get everyone talking but make sure that everyone is included. Find common ground for all of the team members (What vacations are you planning? Have you seen a new movie?) And use it as a five-minute icebreaker each week. Team meetings should happen even if you are not around—make sure someone is set up to be in charge while you are gone. (Tell that person what to do and tell everyone else to contact that person).

If you work in an environment where meetings are more frequent, you may want to differentiate team meetings from project- or problem-oriented meetings. When the team gets together, it's a chance for you to hear about more general concerns, sense the mood in the team, and supply them with information that is not always related to their day-to-day responsibilities. If the atmosphere of the meeting is casual, there is a better chance that you will get honest and open opinions. Don't be afraid to step outside of normal processes with this team meeting—bring snacks, hold it away from the office, and use a room that is not usually part of your routine.

ONE-ON-ONE MEETINGS

One-on-one meetings are necessary too. If your team is relatively small, meet with each person on a weekly basis in a short meeting that is just for the two of you: manager and employee. In person or over the phone, this meeting is useful as an avenue for a communication line that needs to stay open.

MIKE'S MANAGEMENT USE CASE

During a particularly tough time, one of my managers called every day at the same time–just checking in, looking for input, trying to help. At first it seemed overbearing, but he slowly worked his way into the "real" activities between team members and eventually these calls were a lifeline that helped me retain my sanity and stay with the company!

The pressure of everyday work takes away the urgency of many smaller needed actions that you won't hear about or consider until one-on-one time. These items will pile up, especially the personnel-related issues. To get them open for discussion, you have to have a low-pressure time each week when you can just talk. Or rather, during this time you should focus on listening. Let the other person do the talking:

- Bring up discussion topics that were not comfortable for you or the other person in a group meeting. Often, these are interpersonal issues that will surprise you.

- Listen. Listen. Listen. Work to understand concerns that are raised. There are many possible risks when the "floodgates" of individual problems open up, but you will act only on the ones that you judge necessary, and the simple act of listening will make the others seem smaller.

- Implement any reasonable, simple changes that are requested of you, even if they have no real bearing on the work product. This will build confidence in your position as an action-oriented manager.

- Discuss vacation or other personal issues that are pending and will impact the team. Discuss how these should be handled—someone else does the work, work piles up, etc.

- Provide direct, concrete feedback. Negative feedback should be given in private rather than in public.

This is such an important activity that we will dedicate a whole chapter to it later.

- Track long-range goals. Plan how to get employees all of the skills and knowledge they seek to meet their ambitions.

- React to recent events and incidents as a way to coach—help identify problems and work out possible solutions that cannot be discussed in a larger group.

- Obtain feedback on your own work and management style. Ask about your role and value in the person's project, in meetings, etc. This information will not be forthcoming from most of the people you manage, but it is the most valuable information you can find for your career.

PERSONAL PROBLEMS

Have open and honest dialogue in one-on-one meetings to build a relationship of trust. Use information obtained in these meetings carefully and sensitively, always with permission unless a legal or safety concern is at stake. When the discussion becomes personal, which will happen and which will be very unfamiliar to you, focus on professionalism while still listening. Confidentiality is a very easy skill and yet surprisingly few managers demonstrate it fully.

Listening to personal issues may be unfamiliar to you and at first counterintuitive. You may react with the thought that you don't want to deal with nonsense when there is work to do. You may not even be familiar with the life issues that are facing the person you are trying to lead. Regardless, you have to make time for the conversation and you have to make it *important*. You have to understand what is being said by your team member, and even if you don't care about it, you have to factor it into the work plan, risk level, and commitments that you have made.

While some people differentiate strictly between their professional and personal lives, most of us spend so much time at work that we cannot avoid creating personal friendships and bonds with our colleagues. For a manager, it can be nearly impossible to draw a hard line, especially if you manage people for a long time, which inevitably involves joys and sorrows in private life. You may even make close friends among your team or become the manager of people who have been your friends since they were your peers. Professional, balanced, and fair treatment for everyone on the team is still required of you, under all circumstances. Be very honest with yourself and very careful with your emotions.

MBWA

Managing by Wandering Around is a concept introduced by Peters and Waterman in one of the most popular business books ever, *In Search Of Excellence* (1982). As the name suggests, this management technique is extremely simple but surprisingly useful. Think of your own experience under different managers and ask yourself how many of those leaders knew enough about the action within the development team to effectively walk around the work area. Where are the labs? What equipment is used for which services? Who sits in each area, and so forth. It's a sad fact that many managers spend their time away from the people they manage, tucked in offices and meetings, without ever getting out and about where the action really is.

Some very successful companies and even more managers consider Management by Wandering Around *the* most important management technique. For those who practice it, it is easy to understand just how action-oriented the method is: if there is a problem, the manager sees it early and fixes it *immediately* because the experience of seeing the problem in place is *compelling*. As an expected presence because of diligent MBWA, the manager is continuously available and maintains good contact with the team. Even if you do not decide to accept Management by Wandering Around as the primary way to manage your team, we encourage you to perform it during at least some of your time. A good guideline is to be seen frequently enough that your presence does not cause altered behavior; you want to visit your team members in their everyday work life.

MBWA is very different from meetings, and it is the perfect complement to them. MBWA does not guarantee privacy like a one-on-one meeting, but it does allow you to keep in touch one-on-one with a much broader group of people—not only your direct reports but also indirect reports, people from other departments, customers, etc.

MBWA BY THE RULES:

1. Make your visits spontaneous and unplanned, even if you schedule them for yourself to make sure they happen. This supports the feeling of informality. If you make a habit of walking around at the same time each day or on the same day each week, your spontaneous visits will soon be preceded by spontaneous preparations!

2. Don't make them seem like a pop quiz or surprise inspection. You do not want people to wince nervously every time you zoom by. That means you can't turn every flaw or hint of trouble into an impromptu accountability review! Make mental notes but don't carry a notepad.

3. Don't look for problems—instead, look for successes. For example, rather than policing for people who are on long lunches or talking on the phone, find reasons to praise people who are not doing those things. Discuss their issues but do not criticize; you need for people to enjoy your visits.

4. Observe, listen, ask questions, and be genuinely interested. Let people show you what they are working on—and try it out on your own! Sit down with them and explore what they have developed or what they are testing.

5. If you see a problem that you can solve, try to remedy it immediately. This conveys the message that you're here to help. If you can't solve it, coach the situation: suggest alternatives, provide resources to assist, etc.

6. Bring good news if you have any—however simple. Alternatively, explain how the employee's work contributes to the company's vision if it is not clear.

7. Most importantly, have fun and make it apparent that you are enjoying this. Most of the time, you will see the employees making progress and often will be surprised at their creativity and approaches. This could be a rewarding experience for you as well as for the employees.

All of these techniques—team meetings, one-on-one meetings, and management by wandering around—will help you understand better the state of the projects and what the team is currently working on. But what is most important in the light of this chapter is that they will help you maintain contact with the team. Carefully listen and watch for behavior changes. You will be able to identify any morale and motivation problems or any other obstacles to your success much earlier than without this contact.

MANAGEMENT PROGRAM: THINGS TO DO WHEN SOMEONE JOINS YOUR TEAM

- Have a one-on-one conversation with the new person to introduce yourself. Explain who you are and why you are in your role and describe your management process, your current goals, and your expectations.

- Find out about any unfinished activities from the person's previous project, any issues he or she may have outstanding with human resources, any expectations held over from the hiring process or from prior performance reviews if the new person was a transfer.

- Discuss the new person with his or her prior manager, or with the human resources team. Find out about weaknesses that you can avoid or try to strengthen. Find out about motivation and ambitions.

- Assign a mentor for your new team member and ensure both sides understand their responsibilities.

- Consider the project and people with whom the new person is working, determine the best workplace for the new person, and ensure he or she has the right equipment.

- Update project plans and work assignments given the new person's expected contribution.

- Introduce the new team member as a *person* (hobbies, children, etc.) to your existing team in a casual setting such as a meal away from the office.

ー

- Introduce the new person to your team (skills, areas of responsibility, needs for ramp-up assistance) in a formal meeting where updated work plans are laid-out for discussion.

- Work through a ramp-up plan with the new person, starting with learning basic skills and ending with goals that will be used in the first performance review. Look for proactive response from her or him to confirm understanding.

- Follow up one week, one month, and three months later to discuss the experience of initially joining your team, relationships with coworkers and overall satisfaction. Eventually, these follow-up sessions become your ongoing one-on-one meetings with this person.

This may seem really complicated. After all, can't you just greet the new person, have a meeting, and get them productive ASAP by working with an experienced team member? Of course you can. That's an abbreviated process that closely matches the one described above. The point of knowing all the steps to the process is that you know which ones you skipped and why, rather than being surprised sometime later with an unexpected consequence.

MANAGEMENT PROGRAM: THINGS TO DO
WHEN SOMEONE LEAVES YOUR TEAM

- Well in advance of the person's departure, tell your management about the change and the impact it will have.

- Document performance of the person who is leaving up to the point of departure.

- Have a last one-on-one conversation with the person. This is your last chance to get his or her feedback on your performance, on the performance of the team and state of the project. Sometimes this is the most honest feedback you will ever get!

- Reassign work to others on the team (reshuffling priorities if needed). If critical skills are being lost and you cannot shift work around to adapt to this change, then escalate quickly to your manager.

- Have a transition planning meeting where the people with the new assignments have a chance to discuss the current status with the person who is departing.

- If he or she is staying within the company, have a meeting with the employee, and his or her new manager. Share your documentation of performance.

- If other sensitive topics regarding performance need to be communicated, set up a separate discussion with the new manager but without the employee.

- Modify your planning documentation and communicate the impact of the resource lost to your manager and to other teams that are depending on you.

MIKE'S MANAGEMENT USE CASE

The most brilliant engineer I know taught me a simple principle about hitting a deadline. Fundamentally, he says, you have to hit every deadline, from the first milestone to the final delivery, if you are going to finish on time. It seems simple, but examine it from your own experience.

How many software projects can you recall that stuck to a firm deadline for the requirements phase? Compare the number of times that you were on a team that had "crunch time" at the end of a project with the number of times that you had a "crunch time" to hit an intermediate code complete date. The fact is that in software management, a great deal is said about process but intermediate milestones are often not respected.

It's natural to feel pressure on the end dates, when work that we have done becomes external, but it is very easy to blow off intermediate "internal" goal dates because they seem almost arbitrary. The consequence, of course, is that required effort "piles up" on the end dates.

This is a fundamental principle of some of the newer methodologies that work by implementing many short development cycles rather than comprehensive long ones. Plan your milestones carefully with specific goals and dates, and then respect every one of them to level out the urgency that other managers save for heroics at the schedule end.

MANAGEMENT PROGRAM: WHEN YOU ARE GOING
TO PROVIDE FEEDBACK

- When you are involved in a situation that disturbs you, or when you learn about that kind of situation through someone else, first spend some time thinking about it. Determine what, specifically, is the disturbing part and whether it's just your opinion or whether there really is something that requires action.

- Think about what happened (and double-check sources on anything that you did not personally see). Is there a pattern in behavior that is deeper than the specific incident?

- Armed with your distilled thoughts, approach the person involved privately and discuss the specific situation. Remember the old rule of thumb for providing feedback: "Praise in public, coach in private."

- Don't wait too long to have the discussion. The dread that you experience during anticipation is far worse than the actual discussion.

- Explain what you want to talk about, request the person's perspective on the situation and *listen*. Do not accuse the person of anything until you understand how he or she viewed the whole problem and what motivated the behavior in question. You will be surprised how often you will find out that your understanding of the problem was incomplete. Do not make a fool out of yourself by blurting an accusation first, only to find out that you did not have your facts straight.

- Once you get the person's input, explain the problem (assuming there is still one) in the simplest possible terms as a broader pattern, but be prepared to back up your observations with specific examples. What is the policy or value that was violated by the action? Keep in mind that most people, most of the time, don't intend to do things that will require feedback.

- As you are providing feedback, make sure to talk about the person's *behavior* ("you did not find a compromise with your colleagues regarding the change") rather than draw conclusions about *personality or character* ("you are stubborn"). You can hurt people very badly by pointing out their suspected character flaws. But remember that an individual's personality is wholly their own and is therefore not subject to your critique or the company's policies. On the other hand, the company contracts people to deliver certain results and they are expected to behave professionally as part of that contract, so it is perfectly acceptable to discuss what happened in that light.

- Document your thoughts before and after discussions with anyone involved. This will serve you in a few ways: it's material to include in formal reviews; it's a way to find patterns in behavior since you won't always remember details from one incident to the next, and it's a way to provide third parties with necessary documentation if they are authorized to see it.

- Consider engaging human resources. Early on, it's a good idea to discuss most things with someone in HR until you are confident about what to handle alone and what to escalate.

- Always consider what damage was done and how to address it. If you need to provide feedback to someone, it's because something did not go well and therefore something or someone else was impacted. Providing feedback is a way of fixing the problem for the long term, but the short-term consequences need to be repaired too.

UNDERSTANDING PEOPLE

You probably realize that all people are not the same. But you may not realize how different they are, especially if, like most people, you look at others as a reflection of yourself.

To keep people content and motivated in their jobs and maximize results from them, it is crucial to learn their strengths and weaknesses, their likes and dislikes, the structure of their motivation (prestige? money? personal time?), and even their values.

Do not assume that people working for you have the same system of values, opinions, experience, or background that you have. Definitely don't assume they want your values or that you should try to convert anyone from who *they* are to being more like *you*. One person is exhilarated in the design process, before a line of code is written; another one considers any sort of documentation a waste of time that could be spent coding! One is happy when focused on detailed, intense work, while another needs a title and public recognition. One will consider users of the product a mere by-product of his or her genius-level software creation skills, while others will crave interaction with users for their own gratification of a job well done. One will consider his or her desktop equipment a small detail as long as it serves its purpose, while another will feel left out if anyone in the building has a newer model.

Inevitably, some of the team will be more like you, while others will be less so. In fact, someone on your team will be so different that you will have a hard time finding common ground on which to build a relationship. Whatever hand you are dealt, always find something to *like* about each person. Use that as a foundation for a relationship that transcends the day-to-day ups and downs of work. No matter how many levels of management you climb or however frustrated someone makes you, they are still *people* equal to you in all rights and privileges, worthy of your respect and deserving of their own dignity. And if you know the *person*, not just the *worker*, you will be able to sail through even the rockiest times.

MIKE'S MANAGEMENT USE CASE

I was unprepared for the first time that someone on my team broke down and lost emotional control in a meeting with me. I had no concept that my management actions could bring someone to tears because I was too caught up in the power and control that I was feeling as I directed a growing set of people. I had been emotional my-self at times with my own managers, but some-how I did not expect it would happen to me as a manager. It was a very humbling experience!

While I wish I had been better prepared for it, I don't think a manager can ever be completely prepared. People have too many complex, inter-esting, and organic reactions. When things are not going according to the management plan, a good manager has to take a step back and just be a good person. Not to say that managers are not people all the time, but there is a difference be-tween a manager who is "in character," providing praise and direction, and a manager who is just lis-tening and reacting like any other person would.

When someone cannot manage their emotions pro-fessionally, don't push them away because you are uncomfortable. Instead, drop the "boss" angle and find out what's wrong person-to-person. You will have to address the issues "in-character" later, but when you do so, you will have a perspective that will help you decide what to do and take actions to achieve it in a more sustainable, personal way.

In fact, those rocky times are a better test of your "peo-ple power" than the rosy celebrations that emerging managers crave. When you encounter the toughest mo-ments in your relationships with people, remind your-self of the things you know about them to get yourself into a positive mind-set. You cannot provide constructive feedback or coach *anyone* if you are shaking with anger. A negative attitude is *often* hard to contain, and it *feels good* right away to scold someone for something they did. But the workplace is not a traffic accident or a bar brawl, and it is wrong for you to use your authority to berate or reproach a team member! After it happens, and it is likely that it will happen, you will immediately know it was wrong, and your relationship with the person in question will be clouded by the shadow of your reproach for a long time. When that happens, you will experience lower productivity—for yourself and for several others on the team who will all hear every detail about it—and it's *your* fault! It's important to avoid creating this situation, but it's just as important to repair relationships and move on if it happens.

MOTIVATION

People share common character patterns. Because you are a person, like the people you are trying to manage, you can use your own empathy as a guide to management. The ability to recognize and imagine the emotions of others, especially when you have recently been on a team rather than leading one, is a golden capability. Try to understand motivation—how people feel and think, why they do things the way that they do—through clear observation. Set aside the *vision and leadership* that you may have been communicating to your team and just absorb what's actually *happening* to see if people really are motivated.

How to recognize motivated people?

- They voluntarily increase effort if necessary to meet project deadlines and goals.

- They take new challenges with excitement and enthusiasm, preempting any prodding with a flurry of activities such as research, design discussions, etc.

- They work toward the *goals*, not toward process milestones. A good design that solves the business problem is the goal, not just a pretty document one that meets the company standards.

- They look happy at work! This one is easy to see. People smile, they are busy, they walk quickly, and they share resources.

- They give clear and direct answers to questions about their progress. Motivated people are eager to tell you about their goals.

- They accept critique and feedback. Motivated people understand that you are there to help.

If you correctly guess their emotions and motivations and learn to work with them, you can motivate anyone, making their job, and yours, more enjoyable.

CONSISTENCY AND FAIRNESS

One of the manager's hats is to be judge and jury over small conflicts. Rarely will everyone agree on simple things like who gets a new PC first, who gets the window seat, or who will be sent for training this year. Consistency and fairness are important because the team as a whole will disrespect you if you favor someone, or worse, if you are biased *against* someone. Let's be clear—some people will *deserve* and should *receive* more rewards and attention because that's the nature of competition. You will not motivate top performers without top rewards, and some poor performers just won't get the message unless your direct feedback is reinforced by real consequences in your decision-making. You cannot reward and praise everyone equally. Your business demands an environment that rewards talent and effort, promoting improvement and disdaining waste. But there should be a clear and consistent system for how people's performance translates into rewards.

Many situations where fairness is required will be governed by your company policy. Those are the easy ones—learn the policy, enforce the rules—everyone will understand. But when unusual situations arise, your judgment has to engage. What if a high performer is the last person to ask for vacation over a holiday when you can't let the whole department be gone? How about when your equipment budget has run dry but there's one more person without a whiz-bang new monitor that everyone loves? Even Dilbert® cartoons reference well-intended management decisions over apparently trivial things that go wrong, resulting in an avalanche of de-motivation! *Everyone* wants what *anyone* gets, and you must be ready to defend the why's and how's of your policies. You can withdraw and become draconian ("That's it! Nobody gets anything!") or spend hours crafting the ultimate "declaration of developer's rights," but those approaches will fail you in the long term. Instead, think about decisions before you make them and be prepared to respond when challenged. Once your people realize that you have good reasons for all of your actions, they will start bringing you more important things to decide.

YOUR TEAM MEMBERS ARE NOT ALL EQUAL CONTRIBUTORS

This point cannot be emphasized enough because it is so easy for new managers to become worn down with "people issues" to the point of placating everyone. You have to treat people consistently and fairly, but do not make the mistake of treating everyone identically. They are individuals; they have different skills, knowledge, motivation, and character. They behave differently, they produce differently, and they have a different *value* to the project you are managing. People need different rewards—some get guidance, some get control, some get money, some get prestige. All of those are resources that you, as a manager, spend to get the project done.

If you give a hard task to a trustworthy skilled employee and check up on progress a month later, you will find that the work is progressing nicely under the thrill of the challenge, and the level of trust you have provided.

On the other hand, if you do the same with an inexperienced person, you will create despair, confusion, and doubt. A month is far too long for someone who needs your time (coaching, mentoring, and managing) to grow. Motivation is different for these two extreme examples. The necessary level of control and cost to you is different for these two extreme examples. Think about each person on your team in terms of these dimensions and apply yourself accordingly.

Dimensions of people that you should evaluate when considering how to interact with them, assign tasks, and manage them:

- Strengths and weaknesses

- Experience level

- The experience of previous managers

- Unique skills or training

Regardless of how your team members feel, they need different things from you, and it's up to you to decide who gets what. The most obvious decision relates to your level of involvement: what people need from *you* can range from complete trust, delegating fully, to careful step-by-step guidance, also known as micromanagement. Even though micromanagement has negative connotations, it actually is an appropriate technique in some cases!

CLOSURE

People are at the heart of your new leadership role. They need you to set a direction and to keep them on it. They need your attention and your understanding. They will look to you for motivation, information and encouragement. This may be the biggest change for you as you switch career tracks.

Stay in touch with your people in as many ways and under as many circumstances as you can. On-on-one meetings are important, as are group meetings. But meetings won't tell the whole story. You have to get out among your team while they are working to see what is really happening. You will have a more confident perspective, and they will gain respect for your authority.

_____

Chapter 8

DELEGATION

Delegation is a sore subject for many new managers. It's where the proverbial "rubber meets the road" in the role change from being a *developer* to being a developer's *manager*. For the first time, something that used to be *your* job is now someone *else's*. For all of the aspirations and potential in your management future, the act of delegation, to be repeated over and over, is the starting point. In fact, you might as well get really *good* at it!

So what makes it difficult? The biggest pitfall encountered by emerging managers is the instinct to keep too much work for themselves because it is "too important to delegate." These managers fail to realize what it feels like to be on the other side of that decision—in other words, if *important* work stays with the manager, then no one on the team, other than the manager, is *important*. Team members feel left out and trivialized. If you've been paying attention so far, then you know that the manager has failed.

Many developers have their worst management experiences under new managers who have a "star complex." One of our own early experiences under a new manager was a code review that grew more and more ridiculous until the manager deemed that the code simply would not work and needed to be rewritten *on the spot*. The experience was humiliating until a quick compile and test demonstrated that in fact the original code worked on the first try, and the temporary humiliation for the developer became a permanent lesson for the arrogant manager.

Of course, delegation can go very badly as well. Until you gain a lot of experience, delegate but do so carefully and check frequently on the progress that is being made. These checks will help you identify who needs more help and who needs less. Make demands on team members with *empathy* rather than as an imperative. Respect the capabilities of every person, even as you are working with them to improve. Remember, your goal is not to compare yourself to them or to each other but to make all of them deliver their best effort for the team and to grow in the process. Ultimately, you will find that some people do grow under your guidance, while others will fail to muster even a baseline competency. Each person is a different project for you to work on as the manager.

DELEGATION: JUST DO IT

The only task you cannot delegate is management itself. In other words, nothing you do should stop you from making sure your team is busy and productive. As a new manager, you may not have a full-time management workload; if so, you may also contribute to the effort as an engineer or developer. But you can do so only after your management jobs are done! Do not slip into the comfort zone of doing the work yourself.

You are in management because you want to learn to achieve more through a team, not because you want to star on the team.

MAJOR RED FLAG: WHERE IS EVERYBODY?

A story that plays out over and over for each new manager (yes, for both authors as well) is a very dark moment late at night somewhere in the middle of the first big project. The office is empty except for the manager, who has been there for many hours after the cleaning service left. The project is behind schedule, and the manager is working double-time to get the job done. Several other people are on the project, but they can't help. They have all done a great job on their assignments. Still, the manager is exhausted and the weight of the whole project feels crushing. Why can't anyone else help? If this is a group effort, where is everybody? Where is the personal sacrifice from everyone else? This management thing has turned out wrong…

If you are busy and your team members are not, then you are doing something wrong. Why not delegate what you are doing and supervise the results? You have the authority to reorganize the work at any time if it means better results and meta-results for the team. If no one on the team is competent to receive work that you need to delegate, then you are not managing your team's performance or skill set balance. That is acceptable in the short term, but you should be working to improve the team to the point of independence from your individual contribution even as you work to meet the deadline.

You should also introspect for a moment and make sure it is really true that no one else can do the work. Many new managers really want to be the best developers and even unconsciously keep the hardest or most interesting parts of the work for themselves. We've seen this often when eager new managers justify working late into the night as "getting ahead" on the project when in fact what they are doing is humiliating a professional member of their team who is diligently doing the work as assigned, on the schedule that he or she committed.

SLICE AND DICE

Your job is to understand the workload and the skill sets, then break up the tasks and assign them so they reassemble into a completed whole. Deliver the product and grow the people in the process of doing it. You win only when your team members are successful. Your job is to delegate, even if it means you spend the same amount of time (or more!) correcting mistakes as you would doing the work yourself.

If you take time to teach your team while you address issues in their work, you may feel that things are moving at a glacial pace. Remind yourself that, while slow, progress is *accelerating*. That's because you are improving the work of everyone on the team—and they will apply these improvements every day, even when you are not there. Remind yourself that you are expected to get more out of people, to make them efficient, which is exactly what you achieve by teaching.

HONZA'S MANAGEMENT USE CASE

I remember the first project in which I did not assign any tasks to myself. I felt relieved because my workload was becoming too high, but at the same time I was a little uncertain about the future. Will I have enough work to do if all of the sudden I do not have anything specific to deliver myself? What, really, will be my value to the team? Will they think that I am "acting like a manager" and that I got so "full of myself that I think I no longer have to help them"?

All my concerns were unfounded, of course. I had to continue working just as hard as before to keep up with the projects, but I was able to spend much more time with the individual team members. I was better informed and more plugged into the team activities than when I had to spend a large portion of my time coding through parts of the project. I really started *managing* and *leading* the team. If anything, my performance as a manager improved after the change and the team recognized the difference.

You are expected to provide people with a stimulating challenge—impossible if they are not learning. Hopefully, the pattern is becoming clear now. As the manager, your job is to combine your people's need to improve themselves with your company's need for completed projects. The manager brokers delivery of work efforts while creating rewarding careers. It's not easy and it's not for everyone, but it can be done very well and the results are spectacular.

Delegation is especially challenging for emerging managers who came from a background of technical dominance over their teams. The most typical cause of trouble is that they know everyone on the team—warts and all. A strong need to control success will cause new managers to reject every possible person who could be assigned to do the work. The consequence, of course, is that the team will not be able to scale because the manager's own role has a linear relationship to the team's capacity—only so many jobs can be done by anyone other than the manager, so the manager is the bottleneck.

MIKE'S MANAGEMENT USE CASE

I worked with a team of over twenty people that had been organized into a lean machine that could execute a rigid software maintenance process like clockwork. They had a large base of customers who were highly satisfied and the whole operation was quite profitable. The manager oversaw daily activities in detail and even redesigned the office space to flow like the classic stages of requirements, design, code, debug, test, etc.

Then a large commercial event changed the very nature of the work that needed to be done. Previously there was only maintenance work, but now new software had to be created. Where one programming technology was previously used, several new ones were added. Customers once satisfied with one product now demanded three different ones or more.

The manager did his best to adjust but he was trapped. He desperately tried to fit his old assembly-line approach around the new demands of the business. But there were too many concurrent projects and not enough flexibility in the use of different skills and equipment. There were too many details to resolve and only one manager who had ever made a decision. He poured himself into the cracks of longer and longer schedule plans until it became clear that the business was going to fail unless something could be done.

First, the manager had to stop being the bottleneck for the software process because he could not scale to the needs of the business. To do that, he had to nominate team leaders who would establish a degree of autonomy from each other. Next, the teams had to become responsible for their own success or failure, which happened when they took on completely separate projects rather than distinct stages in an assembly line. Finally, the teams needed new skills because they each had to deliver all phases of the development cycle.

It took some time, but far less than expected, to achieve this change. The new team leaders were far too proud of their teams to let them fail.

FACING PROBLEMS

Another syndrome that affects the power of delegation for an even larger group of emerging managers
is their instinct to avoid conflict. These new managers
fear the possibility that an employee who is delegated
a difficult job might do it incorrectly. And, in order to
address the problem, management would be placed
in a difficult situation of balancing the employee's feel-
ings with client needs and date pressures. The emerging manager feels perfectly justified in taking a very
conservative approach—delegating easy goals, over-
resourcing the project, etc. Unfortunately, if the team
is never challenged to learn and grow, you can draw
from your own experience and most likely conclude
that they will not respect their manager and they will
not stay very long with the team or company.

Most of us grow most when we try to overcome an
obstacle that is bigger than our current set of knowledge, skills, and experience. Good delegation is a gift
to your team—give them too much to do and help
them achieve it all! They will like the challenge, and the
respect you gain will cause them to accept whatever
feedback you need to give them along the way.

You want to break up your projects and delegate the
pieces. You want those delegations to turn into goals
that people feel accountable for achieving. And when
it's time for feedback, you want objective facts about
achievements on which to base clear communications. So far, management seems like a formula, but
you know it is not. Delegation and accountability can
be organized on the whole, but every individual action

is creative, complex, and non-intuitive. If you approach it too mechanically, like a math problem, you will fail. For example, you cannot assume that people of similar training and experience will perform equally. If your plan makes that assumption, one person might be underutilized and bored while another is overwhelmed and stressed.

The traditional reference to people as "resources" combined with the technical nature of software development professionals can result in a linear approach that associates one unit of work with one person for a given time period. This approach is wrong and it will lead to failure—specifically your failure as a manager, followed by several other minor disappointments related to projects and customers. That's because the problem is far more complex than a simple linear breakup of assignments. Setting up the right goals for each individual is the *divide* in "divide and conquer." Dividing properly ensures the conquest just as assigning work properly ensures accountability.

STACK THE DECK

If you can, look for a group of individuals you can challenge with absolutely everything that needs to get done. Farm out every bit of your work so that essentially you could set up the assignments and walk away. If you're worried about spending your days with nothing to do, stop worrying right now—your worst case result is getting promoted to a bigger job! By choosing people who will learn and expand their capabilities, you will win supporters that look up to you—after all, you entrusted them with responsibility, which leads to growth. Even one or two people who have a positive outlook about growth and change are sufficient to challenge and improve everyone on a team. And because they are learning, you will help people become competent while making the whole project a lower-risk effort. The results are positive all around even though the risk-averse approach beforehand would have predicted otherwise.

THE TORTOISE AND THE HARE

A frequent reason for a failure to delegate is when an emerging manager says, "I can do it faster myself." While it is often true that one person can do one job faster than another person can do that same job, it is a very short-sighted gain. This kind of approach leads to exactly the same de-motivation as other failures to delegate. In fact, this reasoning is a major de-motivator for top performers who try to move into management, fail to delegate, find themselves overworked, and decide they hate management even though they never really did it!

Initially, the manager may be a faster worker than one or two people, or even the whole team, but sooner or later, if the team is motivated and growing, that same team will blow the manager away. The catch 22 is that, until the manager stops doing all the work and starts delegating, the team won't improve. The point is that you should be *teaching* while making corrections to work that you delegate. At some point, the efficiency curve will tip in your favor and from then on the training will pay off *every day*. You are expected to get more out of people to make them efficient. You are expected to provide people with a stimulating challenge. As the manager, your job is to combine these two, brokering delivery of work products while creating stronger assets for future efforts.

NO SAFETY NET

Savvy emerging managers, especially experienced professionals, cite another reason to avoid delegation: fear of obsolescence. Either because they want to keep their technical skills sharp or because they want to retain some level of security through association with clients or by directly *creating output*, these managers fail to delegate. Their motivation is noble—certainly technical skill and product knowledge are *great* aspirations for management. But what they fail to realize is that their safety net will cause them never to give up the individual contributor role, and they will, therefore, never really focus on management as a competency. In fact, because they view a direct contributor role as a fallback position, they never really commit to management.

If you really want to emerge as a manager, you have to make your success depend on using new and different skills. Use your *team* to get the job done, while *you* make sure the team is healthy and improving. You can still be very well informed about what is happening every day, and you can still even do some of the day to day work. But prepare to see and understand fewer details while seeing more of the overall picture—this will be the trend as you progress within any organization.

MIKE'S MANAGEMENT USE CASE

Something that surprised me over and over again in the early management days was that I kept meeting more and more new people. As a developer, I would occasionally meet a new co-worker but that was about it. Once I took on leadership roles, it seemed the parade of people who needed to meet me would never end. HR, executives, product managers - It was a big distraction to have to deal with email, calls and drop-ins from all over the place.

Then I realized that I had started to get useful information from some of those people. They shared market information or client rumors; they gave me scheduling insight for production and technical support programs, and so on. Even some of the things that I had previously ignored like company financials started to click for me. More importantly, they were related to what my team was doing.

I was surprised to find many other people with the same challenges and joys that I was experiencing. There were managers who needed to know more about what I was doing so they could plan better, and vice-versa. Deadlines like accounting milestones became real priorities once I knew the person who set them, and why. Production delivery of software had been a huge mess but we worked it out once I met the person on the receiving end. It was not without frustration but I became part of a much bigger group of managers from all functions in the company. Things from outside of software development became interesting and important as I never knew they could be.

WE DON'T NEED ANOTHER HERO

If you want to manage, you have to avoid the risk of becoming indispensable in your current position. You cannot move up in the organization if you are irreplaceable at what you do now. This is a complex issue for individual contributors. How can you become very good at your technical job in the short term if doing so will stop you from advancing in the long term? Let's break the problem down further.

The best individual contributors are the ones who have the ability to set a goal and predictably achieve it. They understand the technical domain well enough to predict their own work effort, foresee obstacles and overachieve when needed. These are *heroes* in our jargon. Heroes have found a niche in the software engineering ecosystem, and they thrive in it as the top predator of their world. These heroes are often the only people who are capable of salvaging a client relationship or averting a major disaster. They are deservingly powerful people.

The tragedy of the hero is that more and more is demanded of that person because he or she demonstrates the ability to achieve things that apparently cannot be done through management of "big teams."

Because of the dominance of the hero, no one else develops similar expertise. The hero dutifully overcomes the lack of competent assistance by pouring him or herself into the work at hand instead of training others to do it. Management, and even customers, is often willing to be very careful with the hero's time, adding to the cachet of the hero's role.

But there are only so many ways this can end:

- Eventually the technology becomes obsolete and, since the hero had no time to build a replacement, the hero becomes obsolete along with it.

- Demands mount higher and higher, and the hero, in due course, burns out.

- The workload finally enlarges beyond the hero's capabilities. It becomes necessary to work around the hero, eventually replacing him or her forcibly for the good of the business.

- The hero emerges as a manager. He or she demands ninety days' reprieve and a staff of three people to train. A star is born.

If you want larger responsibilities, don't put yourself in the critical path of the ones you have now. This may seem counterintuitive, but in fact, it is central to the idea of leadership and management. Yes, you should work hard and be dependable. You should take on larger assignments and grow your skills. But always welcome opportunities to show others what you do. Gently and constructively review other people's designs and code every chance you get. Document your efforts in detail so others can easily extend what you do. Refactor old code, using new technology so your product evades obsolescence. These are all great practices that you already know about. But the unforeseen benefit for you is that by following them, you can do a great job, avoid becoming a hero with a dead-end tragic career, be a role model, and open new avenues for yourself—all at once!

If you are not persuaded, think of it a different way. If you are the only one who can perform certain functions, then you are limiting how much of that function can be done at any one time. You are stopping other people from learning that function. You are making everyone dependent on yourself, which is disempowering to everyone else as they go about their jobs. Being too possessive of a deliverable or a specific skill may seem like the right way to demonstrate "ownership" over an area of competence. Like many errors in technical careers, it feels like the right noble approach to "jump on the grenade" and save the day every chance you get.

You may even expect management responsibility to follow your possessive approach. After all, if you are the expert, new people should report to you, right? The reality is that your time is too precious and so you will in fact be removed from the opportunity for management so that you can work more. It will be assumed that you would prefer to stay at the individual contributor level and that you would be demoralized if asked to make a move into management.

DELEGATION AND ACCOUNTABILITY

Another counterintuitive change during a manager's emergence is the idea of remaining accountable for things even when other people are doing them. As individual contributors, we are so used to the idea of possession—we have skills, we have work assigned, we have achievement for completing the work with our skills. We use possessive terminology for these things because we really do feel that they are *ours* (my job, my career, my training). Management is just like that, but one level of indirection further away—you have people with skills, you assign them work, and you are responsible for what they achieve on your behalf.

Saying that you are accountable for your team's results is not the same thing as saying that your team members are not. Quite the opposite! For delegation to be successful, you must use and build a culture of accountability with every individual and on every level. Most people naturally grasp that they are responsible for their own work, but you will run into some who will have to be reminded of that fact. When you explain that you feel responsible for the team's performance, they may immediately feel relieved of that responsibility. Somehow, they believe that you are solely in charge of their goals, results, and career growth. These individuals clearly do not understand their own role, or yours as the leader. Work closely with them in a positive manner until you feel that they are aligned.

Unlike technical problems, delegation is a fuzzy, *qualitative* challenge. You have to make decisions about which resources are capable of taking on pieces of the work with many different dimensions to consider. You have to consider the people who can receive work from you—their seniority, skills, and autonomy.

MIKE'S MANAGEMENT USE CASE

I was fortunate to hire a very capable new grad in one of my first management roles. I thought I would give him a simple project for a couple of weeks to get him started. He got off to a great start and had what I needed done in a week, so I asked him to wrap it up with some documentation and a final code check-in.

One week later, he had converted the user interface to color and added some user-friendly features that I liked, so once again, I asked him to wrap it up.

At the start of week three, he had rewritten it in a new environment and it was almost working so he wanted more time. I should have said no, but I wanted to support him—he got the extra time but I was very specific about what he needed to get done.

Cutting to the chase, he spent a total of two months to over engineer a simple utility because I was not managing him closely. As a new graduate, he was very capable of his work but as a new manager, I was not capable of mine. We would have both been more effective if I had given him better guidance, more frequently. After even one year of experience, he would not have let this project drag out so long, but it was my responsibility to manage him before he had that judgment.

You have to measure out portions of your own time and avoid becoming the bottleneck to your own success. To make matters worse, every part of this delicate system is changing—projects change, people change, and you emerge further and further into management. Accountability is like a constraint on the whole process; it is a way for you to stay focused on your goals. It is easy to miss an opportunity to improve the outcome or to eliminate a wasteful effort without the notion of accountability to guide you.

For many people who consider a management role, the idea of being held accountable is a choking prospect—like a thick cloud hanging over the future of their careers. That is a healthy initial response to the idea of management because it implies a heavy sense of responsibility. Managers who feel this way will serve their teams and companies well. But this image can be debilitating in the long run, and it has to be shed quickly because it could stop the new manager from being bold enough to conquer obstacles and lead with vision. Instead, accountability should be thought of as a guide, a clear way of always knowing which direction to go with any decision. You will not be burned at the stake or even fired when you make your first few mistakes in management. In fact, if you simply have more successes than failures, you will most likely continue to be given greater challenges.

When you are in charge, you have to harness all of your accountability fears into useful energy to create urgency and importance for your project. Nobody else will do so for your team, which is another very hard change to undergo when you become a manager. Within the scope of what you are responsible for doing, there are one thousand ways to be successful, and many more ways to fail. *Leadership* is choosing one of these ways with sound logic and sticking to that logic until new knowledge indicates the need to change. You won't hear from anyone about what a great job you are doing. You have to be confident in your own vision to tell yourself that you are on the right course. It's lonely at the top!

Approach delegation like any other occasion when you set a goal. Make sure that the goal is complete, clear, unambiguous, and specific, and that both sides understand by when and with what resources it has to be achieved, and how the progress will be controlled.

THE MORE THE MERRIER

Here's a surprise: Most people perform best when they feel that they have a lot of work to do. A "near over-load" appears to help software engineers prioritize clearly, work succinctly, and drive sensible urgency. They do not feel underutilized or unchallenged. Of course, this is not true for everyone, and certainly you can overload people, even with the noble intent of helping them to grow. Especially with inexperienced team members, you will find that they are quickly overwhelmed, so gauge carefully by observing and checking results.

MIKE'S MANAGEMENT USE CASE

A very senior developer joined my team, so I had a goal-setting session with him to set our mutual expectations. As a key contributor in other areas, he was accustomed to being given broad instructions and latitude to achieve results. I respected his level of accomplishment and determined worthy goals for my team that he could support.

We were off to a good start until the discussion turned to time lines. He was uncomfortable being accountable for doing specific things on or before specific dates. In fact, he considered it disrespectful given his track record; according to his view, I should not treat the creative process of his work as if it were manual labor. We agreed to disagree at first and met a few times to hash it out. I was accountable for getting commercial business results from him in exchange for providing him with a meaningful and rewarding job. That equation had to be balanced, and I held my ground until he and I could come to agreement.

He became a technical mentor for two team members and multiplied their talents through his own, an experience that he previously did not have. He also learned to engage with business managers to define functionality, an area he previously considered outside his own capability.

DELEGATION BY THE RULES

1. Stretch the individual's capabilities without risking the program. To solve this problem, assign work to teams whose members can support each other and learn in the process.

2. Give each individual enough security by giving each enough "slam dunk" work to keep them confident in their value and contribution. When a person can show progress on some part of his or her workload while struggling with more complicated "stretch" goals, that person will stay centered without losing hope. You may find that you have to add useful filler tasks that are not absolutely critical to your project in order to create this environment. For example, encourage team members to remain partially engaged (consultation only! No deliverables) with previous responsibilities, where their expertise is accepted and praised.

3. Give everyone on the team some aspect of the overall work that is important and urgent. As a manager, you create these circumstances by the way you frame the assignment with the individual and by the way you emphasize it to the group. You create urgency. You define the vision. Include everyone in it!

4. Give everyone on the team work that they want to do, that they can be proud to do. The key to

> this step is allowing people to choose which parts of a solution they want to deliver. There are many parts to any project, so everyone must take a different part.
>
> 5. Remember, you only have so many people and so many tasks. Don't get stuck trying to build a perfect world (according to rules 1, 2, 3, and 4). At the end of the day, you have to divide, assign, and conquer. Set it up and let it run.

DELEGATING DECISIONS

Just as you delegate tasks, you can also delegate decisions. Do not fall into the trap of deciding everything yourself—it's a form of bottleneck that is particularly debilitating to the team. Instead, delegate day-to-day decisions about things that others can evaluate better anyway. Delegate decisions about things you would want the team to handle when you are not available. You want your team to feel like they actually can make decisions; they control their own destiny. After all, remember that the organization chart is upside down—you set them up, they deliver the result. Of course, be careful to avoid creating frustration and helplessness if no one has the skills or necessary information to correctly make needed decisions. Let the team go on as long as they can without you and step in with the most subtle guidance you can possibly add while still solving the problem.

Be prepared to disagree with decisions that you delegated. When this happens, hold back your instinct to overrule; doing so would have a devastating effect on any future authority that you try to delegate. Instead, discuss the decision and try to explain what would have been a *better* decision. You will get more respect when you let the team "fix" the problem with very light guidance from you, and the learning experience will be significant. Of course, if your authority is challenged or if team members shrug off accountability ("OK, well if you want it that way, then I can't get my part done. Sorry."), you should be very explicit about actions that need to be taken to address the problem.

A FINAL WORD

As a last word on this topic, remember that the job done well is a continuous stream of decisions and communication that can be intensely exhausting at first. The business pressure comes in the form of large projects, which are often ambiguously defined. The manager's role is to divide and conquer. How he or she chooses to do this will mean the difference between success and failure. If management is achieving results through other people, then good delegation is the beginning of good management.

But don't try to hold a team member accountable for something that you know is his or her weakness. If you set the person up for a failure, expect a failure. If you are experimenting, accompany the person and drive it together—fail together and *teach*. Balance this "care and feeding" approach against the need to stretch people; learn to recognize when someone really has a limitation and when you simply don't want to risk asking him or her to go beyond it.

CLOSURE

Delegation takes practice. Sometimes you don't know how to tell someone what to do without insulting their intelligence or feeling like a bully. Sometimes you get so frustrated that you think you would rather just do the work yourself. Other times, when the planets align, you have a whole team running so smoothly that you feel like a genius.

In time, delegation is a skill that will come with ease and grace. Until then, your team will be patient if you remain fair, admirable and listen to their needs. But don't hesitate to delegate – the only thing you can't delegate is management itself.

———

Chapter 9

COACHING

Your team is most likely full of highly skilled individuals who have a similar background to your own, and they each want to solve big problems by breaking them down into smaller pieces. They most likely do not mind solving the small issues, but they must have a chance to work on the big picture too. They have brains, intelligence, initiative, and motivation. Unless you take it away from them, that is.

Coaching is a management style that is focused on aligning the individual team members' goals with the whole team's goals. It is based on the understanding that if you can positively challenge people and allow them to grow by being in charge of big and important goals, rather than being buried in simple repetitive tasks, their motivation will skyrocket. People are perfectly capable of achieving team goals if they feel empowered to do so and are motivated by their own individual opportunity to win.

WHAT COACHING *IS NOT*

Let's have a look at an example to better understand the different approaches to team leadership. All the product and people names that follow are fictitious;

they are not intended to represent any actual names from the world outside of these examples. Let's start with team A, led by Alan. Alan is a very skilled developer. In fact, he is at least as skilled as each of his team members, plus he has a proven success record and rich experience in the products of the company. Alan's team is tasked with development of a new reporting subsystem for a commercial product that the company sells. It could be anything, so replace this work with your own example if that helps.

Alan had a solution the very minute he was given the task and could not wait to step before his team:

Alan: Guys, I have great news. Because we did so well on the last two projects, we were given a new challenge that could not be given to just any other team in the company. We will develop a Web reporting application for CaseDevil. I sketched the design already and here it is—we will basically build a Petadata warehouse next to the existing Profet OLTP database and develop ETL to fill it. We can use the security model from CaseDevil, which stores all security information in LDAP anyway; for the reporting engine we will use Diamant Reports running on top of PSA.TEN. Here are the rough hosting sketches and the initial scope of the project. I took a shot at a project plan—it looks like we should deliver version one in three months. Do you have any questions?

…long silence.

Alan did his homework well. But it would be false to think that the people in the room have identified themselves with the project after his monologue. It will take Alan a long time for anyone on the team to feel truly empowered on this project because he has established so clearly that he is the expert. Team members will get individual assignments based on the project plan; they will complete their work, but they will not feel responsible because they did not decide anything. For example, if it is eventually determined that Diamant Reports was not really the best reporting engine to use, Alan's name will be invoked over and over. When, after three months, it becomes evident that the project is off schedule, the team will not rally to the deadline because it was not their design, their estimate, or their opinion. They were drafted into a boxed-in role for which they will not be passionate. The manager did not align their personal goals with the project. No one will grow during this project, though the product might be delivered with high quality and on time.

THE ALTERNATIVE

Team B is led by Bob. Bob is just as good a developer as Alan, but he also has the reputation of being a great coach. When Bob steps in front of his team, the situation looks rather different.

Bob: Team, I have great news. Because we did so well on the last two projects, we were given a new challenge that could not be given to just any other group. We will develop a Web reporting application for CaseDevil. We are being asked how fast we can get it done, so we should come up with something. What do you think?

Peter: Well, that's easy—I did reports in my last com-
         pany, and we were using PastV Reports for that.
         It was all pretty simple, but preparing the layouts
         was painful; it took a lot of time and maintenance;
         it was tedious. When marketing got their hands
         on it at one point, we did nothing but change
         colors and fonts in the reports for two months.

Bob: That does not sound too good. What did you do
         to fix it?

Peter: Well, we never did anything about it because
         there was no time to refactor. But I thought
         about it, and we could build something like a
         Report Style Manager to maintain the report
         styles, especially if we are going to go inter-
         national and have to localize and customize it
         over and over around the world.

Bob: Yes, that might be worth doing.

Peter: And I also had the idea of doing my own script lan-
         guage to define report layouts. Then you would
         basically code the layout and would not have to
         draw it.

Bob: That sounds complicated… what is the benefit?

Peter: Well, you would basically "code" the reports in-
         stead of laying out those little squares, which
         are really annoying in the shrink-wrap version.

Alice: But then the end users or consultants won't be
         able to do the report layouts unless we teach
         them the language.

Bob: Yes, that is actually a valid point. We should consider that. Peter, you are saying that the biggest problem was laying out the report elements?

Peter: Yes, you have to align them and everything. It is a lot of boring work.

Alice: And how about the Diamant Reports? I read that they had released a new version that seems to have a lot of new stuff. I would swear they have styling and tables, which allow you to lay out the whole report really quickly. We can't be the first people to ever need to do this! Why recreate the wheel?

Peter: I have never worked with that, but we should check it out. Let's go online after lunch.

Bob: OK, let's do that. Peter, you seem to have the most experience with designing reports. Will you look at the Diamant Reports and tell us whether they solve the problems you observed with PastV Reports?

Peter: I would love to. I am really curious how far they got. Alice, do you want to be in on this too?

Alice: Absolutely. I never did any reporting, but I am eager to learn more about it.

Bob: Excellent. Now, Peter, tell us more about the report development.

Peter: Sure. You basically have to prepare the data—we mostly did it by writing SQL, against the existing database. Then, you prepare the report layout, which is like drawing on a page, and bind the data to the report. It works beautifully.

Bob: Hmm, it may also be a problem to run the queries on the existing databases in production. We know the other teams are sensitive to that. If we expect to publish the information online for everyone who has access to the system, we won't be able to control the traffic.

Carl: Exactly. FlibittyTec has been having huge problems with their database performance. If we start running some new reports now on top of that, it'll kill their systems.

Bob: Yes, and the requirement is to be able to keep five years of history for reporting.

Peter: Phew, that will be a lot of cases!

Alice: Perhaps we won't have to store the individual cases, and we will be able to aggregate the data.

Carl: You mean build our own warehouse?

Alice: Yes!

Bob: That is a really cool idea, and it should scale very well.

The discussion will go on and on. Bob will slowly assemble the whole system with the team. They will talk about the individual pieces and how difficult it will be to put them together. They will discuss options and pick the best ones. They will kill bad ideas and focus on the good ones. People will contribute ideas and get excited about them.

Together they will create confident estimates. (Bob will then add his own buffer because he knows that estimates created in the initial excitement are always wrong!) These will be estimates that came from the team for their own work so everyone will support the schedule that Bob proposes. They will pick assignments based on what they would like to work on. Most of them will choose things that they thought up during the brainstorming because they feel responsible and excited about that part of the work. The discussion with Bob's team will probably take much longer than Alan's "presentation," but Bob's team will leave the meeting with a much better understanding of the system, the project and their role in it.

So does this mean that Bob did not have to prepare and that he had the team do all the work? Yes and no. Bob had to think about this quite a bit before stepping in front of his team. He had to have a fairly good idea of what he would like the team to achieve. He may even have had the complete picture of the system in his head, but he resisted the temptation to blurt it out. He let the team interact to find the solution so they could feel empowered and enthusiastic during the following weeks of work.

Bob had to stay alert during the whole discussion, ask the right questions, fend off bad ideas in a way that led the team members to realize that the ideas were bad, and suggest alternatives. Bob had to support good ideas and help them develop. He had to help the team realize the full scope of the problem and make sure nothing got left out. Bob had to pull the wallflowers out into the discussion and tame the chatty talkers so that others could speak.

Bob got the team exactly where he wanted them to go—a prototype design with individuals excited to sponsor the pieces. He knew they would have ideas and sometimes even deep insight into the problem.

COACHING A WHOLE TEAM

In the team-coaching approach, an emerging manager lets the team distribute the assignments among themselves. The coach provides a description of the problem and the constraints (time line, quality, etc.) and then challenges the team to support each other in achieving the overall goal.

This is a non intuitive change for a strong technical mind. The emerging manager must focus on presenting the goal rather than devising a solution—but so many instincts still command just the opposite! The manager must focus on people and what opportunities can be created for them, suppressing any desire to tackle the puzzle directly. In the end, this approach achieves a number of benefits:

- Allows individual choice of specialization within the team. If someone wants to be "pigeonholed," then he or she can choose that; if not, then the person can choose a variety of assignments.

- Allows people to set or break through their own limitations. Rather than you establishing the capabilities of the people on the team, you allow them to choose their own limits. If team members believe you are fair and informed, then they will stretch themselves for you and for the company. That is because they believe you are representing an important goal, and you know how to help progress their career.

- Delivers the strongest performance by the most people. Your team members will choose the areas that they are most passionate about, and people are best at the things that hold their passion. In addition, because the team chose their assignments, they will be focused to deliver on their commitment.

- Provides a platform for you to coach performance. If the team encounters difficulties, the emerging manager will have a simplified job delivering performance-enhancing feedback given that each person chose the assignment and "signed up" to complete it. Make sure that the feedback you provide is helpful and inspiring—offer help, encourage other team members to get engaged. But don't allow anyone to back out of a commitment unless he or she is simply incompetent.

- Builds a future team. As an emerging manager, you were most likely handed a team that had previously not functioned as a unit. After the first project with you, they will know each other's personalities, strengths, abilities, and habits. The value of this interpersonal relationship network cannot be overemphasized—you will be able to get the same team to commit and deliver more after they have succeeded once.

META-RESULTS OF COACHING

Coaching helps people reach their goals through encouragement and gentle guidance. Coaches do not give direct orders but rather inspire others to find their own insights and solutions. Coached team members are committed to achieve goals and readily accept accountability for completing them. The coach motivates, supports, discusses, and asks open-ended questions.

Consider these meta-results of coaching:

- It builds self-sufficient individuals and teams who are capable of making decisions on their own and who can quickly react to change.

- It helps people identify with their goals because of a fundamental understanding rather than a corporate mandate.

- It teaches employees responsibility for their decisions and actions.

- It creates an atmosphere of support and trust.

- It teaches management about alternative opinions and ideas.

To achieve all of that, good coaches use some common techniques:

- They establish a relationship of trust with their team. A coach demonstrates a genuine interest in each person's career and future. Coaches respect every opinion and respond supportively to failure.

- Coaches do not "give orders" without a thorough understanding of the circumstances. Instead, coaches work with the team and team members to understanding the challenges and goals until everyone has the same clear picture of how to proceed.

- Coaches do not provide finished solutions but instead help create an environment that fosters the creation of solutions.

- Coaches ask the right questions. Open-ended questions allow the coach to direct a discussion without throttling creativity. A coach is an active listener who learns when to let a discussion continue and when to nudge it with a suggestion or a question. Active listening is in itself a great life skill that is well documented in books and online sources.

- Coaches help the team solve problems by providing guidance through the problem-solving process. A coach promotes brainstorming and exploration of alternatives at the right time, but then systematic analysis and closure when all avenues have been reasonably exhausted.

- Coaches provide continuity and discipline by following up on tasks that were taken on by each person. The coach provides feedback quickly when projects go off course. A coach knows that a constructive confrontation early on can relieve a world of problems down the track.

- Coaches celebrate success.

As you can see, coaching is much more demanding than the traditional "just do what I tell you" approach, in terms of time, patience, and communication skills. There will be moments when no matter how hard you try, you will not be able to steer someone toward a solution that you would consider acceptable. At other times, the schedule simply won't allow enough time for great coaching. As the manager, you decide when to use coaching and when it is not appropriate.

COACHING INDIVIDUALS

All that has been said about coaching teams applies just as well to individuals. In fact, team coaching is nothing but coaching a group of individuals all at once. The coach must still recognize every member's individual value, contribution, and personal need for growth, rather than treat the whole group as a set of units which are capable of producing a certain amount of output per hour.

Coaching people one-on-one is more intimate and personal. Issues can be discussed more openly than in a group setting, but the goal and techniques used are unchanged. You are still trying to maximize the individual's potential and opportunities, understand motivation, present worthy and challenging goals, and build mutual trust. The means to that end are listening, open questions, honest feedback, praise, and dialog.

Include coaching in your management toolbox and you will be surprised how much you will learn about your people and how much respect you will gain for them. Most people have talents, knowledge and skills that you will never uncover if you do not have that kind of dialog.

RISKS OF COACHING

Coaching comes with some risks, especially for a new manager. The most likely pitfalls you could encounter are these:

- Over commitment. Team members either strive too hard to impress you or else they are not mature enough to know their own strengths. They choose to take on too much, and they cannot deliver. First and foremost, the emerging manager is monitoring progress for everyone on the team, ensuring that if there is an over commitment problem, it is discovered as early as possible. One often-cited situation is that someone who takes on a task subsequently disagrees with the design, scope, or estimate to completion. When this happens, obviously it's time for a recovery strategy.

- Some work remains after everyone on the team is fully occupied. In this situation you may legitimately have a resource shortage, but before you escalate this to your manager, look into the details. Are the tasks that remain to be done a higher priority than other tasks people signed up for? If so, ask for volunteers to swap.

- Some people on the team may "sandbag" you. That means they knowingly commit to achieve less than they should. Sandbagging can happen when individuals have too many activities outside of the manager's control, or when they lack motivation to achieve their best. If you suspect that this is happening to someone on your team, have a private discussion with that person. Make sure they realize that your expectations are based on their current position and salary, and that upcoming performance appraisals will be based on their contribution. You may find yourself in a recovery mode before you even start the project, but don't worry—it's all part of how you emerge as a manager.

Once the goals are set, it is your job to monitor progress, measure performance, and provide feedback. You have to identify problems and provide mitigating actions, remove barriers and keep motivation high. You must establish the right communication channels within the team and beyond. Every success should be publicized and celebrated—don't miss a single one and be twice as jubilant when anything is done earlier than expected. You are building the reputation of each team member and of the team as a whole; don't wait too long or let an accomplishment slip by you because you think it is too small.

CLOSURE

Coaching is a management style that few other approaches can match. It provides deep benefits to you, your team, and your products. The central idea is to engage people in the decision-making processes related to their work, goals and personal development. Plans made in this way will be more likely to succeed because the person affected by each decision feels responsible for a positive outcome.

Coaching won't work for every circumstance, and it has the downside of putting you in a tough spot if your team disagrees with what you know must be done. But the benefits, especially for the long term, are worth the risk.

———————

Chapter 10

DIFFICULT SITUATIONS

A number of different circumstances in the work of a manager fall into a category that we call "difficult situations." These are interpersonal, nontechnical moments in which a manager must control outcomes if there is to be progress for the team, project, or company. Some of the difficult situations are confrontations; some of them simply require communication of an unwelcome message. These situations arise regardless of what kind of project, process, or company is involved. And, like many other aspects of the transition into management, they are often an unfamiliar and undesirable component of the new role.

As an engineer or software developer, you were probably isolated from difficult situations that would distract or stress you. If your leadership was up to par, your manager was keeping you efficient and productive by eliminating roadblocks and distractions. But the downside is that now, as you emerge into management, you have little or no experience dealing with those things. Your first role leading people will be a crash course that will educate you very quickly. Here are the kinds of things you can expect:

- Difficulty between team members—technical disagreements or, worse, harassment or performance complaints

- Difficulty between yourself and a team member—simple things, like "Can I have a raise/promotion?" or complex ones, like "Why should I work for you!"

- Inappropriate behavior by a team member—surfing the Internet or distracting other people, dress or hygiene issues

- Performance problems—low attendance, late deliverables, low quality.

We encounter difficult situations all the time, and with experience, they begin to feel as natural as technical discussions. Before then, they can wreck a management career unfairly. Every aspect of these confrontations is full of stress and downsides:

- Anxiety during anticipation of an upcoming confrontation or delivery of a difficult message. This anxiety can be distracting, often impacting other areas of the manager's performance. It can also lead to avoidance, perpetuating a problem longer than necessary. The consequences of facing an issue head-on may temporarily be worse than just continuing to tolerate the problem but you have to choose the right time and step up to the plate. Many emerging managers fail because they remain paralyzed waiting for a spontaneous solution that never comes.

- Poor communication during the situation itself. The message never seems to come out right, degrading the confidence of the manager when in fact the outcome is as good as the circumstance will allow (remember, the situation is not your fault—the solution is your chance to achieve).

- Post confrontational replay. The manager dwells on difficult situations, replaying them over and over, trying to understand what was said and why. Oftentimes, the replay process is a search for logic and reason, but in fact interpersonal situations are often not governed by these. Like other parts of becoming a manager, this is difficult!

MIKE'S MANAGEMENT USE CASE

A brilliant developer on another manager's team was well respected for his technical capabilities. His work was so important to the success of some projects that he was treated with "kid gloves" and never reproached for any reason. He enjoyed his status and avoided blatantly abusing it until he discovered...shorts.

Well outside of company policy, wearing shorts was considered too informal for our business environment, but this brilliant developer began wearing them every day anyway. Before long, many others joined the irresistible dress code mutiny.

The CEO would have none of it. He came down on the director of product development because the environment had become too casual for our facility! Many one-on-one discussions were held that very afternoon and most people were back to long pants the next day.

But no one wanted to discuss this issue with the genius who started it all...what if he became angry and decided to stop performing or quit? Any manager who caused that problem would be drawn and quartered.

I solved the problem specifically by not making it a "big deal." I waited until I had a semiprivate hallway crossing with the perpetrator and pointed to his bare legs while saying, "Who invited them out?" He smiled back and said, "I was wondering how long I could keep it up. I guess you got picked to fix it? Well, consider it done." And it was.

Some amount of anxiety is productive in these circumstances. It is a natural way of ensuring that you focus on the situation and resolve it in the most fair and unbiased way possible. However, it is not healthy or useful to dwell needlessly, constantly revising your plan or agonizing over something you should have said. There is no correct formula for how to deal with one of these situations, but there is a reasonable process to follow:

- Gather all possible information you can related to the problem. Take care not to exacerbate the issue by asking everyone about it, such as might happen if you prompt people with a leading question.

- Describe the problem in the simplest possible way for yourself, but do not assume that you understand the situation fully until you have a chance to talk with the offender and understand his or her point of view.

- Consult experts. More experienced managers will help define the problem and possible solutions. Human resources will help you decide which solution is appropriate in the case of problems with people. If you are dealing with sensitive information about any person, be careful not to spread this information around as you search for advice. It is perfectly normal to share all information with people who are your direct superiors, or with human resources. But others should receive only absolutely necessary information, and without personal facts.

- Formulate a desired outcome or resolution. You are going to take action(s) to resolve a problem. What is the outcome that you want to achieve? You can transform a problem into an advantage, eliminate it, work around it, neutralize it, etc.

- Define actions needed to achieve the outcome. This should be the hardest part because it is your opportunity to emerge as a great manager. It is the preparation for execution steps that will follow. Define what has to happen and in what order, involving who, and so forth. Carefully plan communications with people, rehearsing specific messages if you need to do so with your spouse or with a friend. Use role-play as a tool to prepare for difficult meetings of any kind. Think about what you will say and what responses or challenges you could receive. You will be surprised how hard the rehearsal is and how easy it makes the actual meeting.

- Validate your plan with the experts. Again, senior management and human resources are the people who can help you. If you have prepared well, not only will you solve a problem, but you will also impress them and build your own career. Solving difficult problems is not a desirable activity, but doing it well is very important. Unless otherwise recommended, avoid the temptation to offload the problem onto a superior who has more experience. You've done all the work, you need to finish it.

- Complete the required actions as you defined them. Work from planning documents. Communicate confidently because of your planning. Stick to the plan unless the fundamental facts change.

- Evaluate the results. Learn from what happened. For any part of your plan that did not happen as you expected, think about the situation and make yourself notes for the next opportunity.

LEGAL NOTICE

Interpersonal situations can have legal ramifications. As a manager, you are supervising people and that means they have a very different relationship to you than when they were your peers. Your authority creates a different context for your words and deeds. Consult human resource professionals when considering how to interact with

---

people if you are carrying a difficult message. Discuss the situation, the action you plan to take, and seek guidance on both how to convey the message as well as your legal responsibilities. If your difficulty is with a specific person who has encountered ongoing problems with other managers, make sure you are speaking to the human resources representative who has followed this issue in the past. You will most likely not be given information related to previous problems; don't worry—this is not a question of your authority but rather of the individual's personal privacy.

Like many other aspects of taking on a role in management, the topic of legal ramifications can be daunting. You should be concerned and you should be careful. But don't be so concerned as to stop yourself from moving forward in a management career. Get educated about what you can do and how to do it. Be considerate of everyone, always, because they are people above all. And do the job—communicate the tough message, implement the required change, take the leadership position, and do the right thing.

OFF THE MAP

It would be impossible to list all of the troubles you may get into in your role as a new manager. Performance management difficulties are virtually guaranteed so that category has its own section later on. But so many other situations are possible that you'll eventually fill your own book of anecdotal experiences. Here are some principles that have proven useful to us:

- What's done is done. It's not useful to engage in elaborate debates and what-ifs about past situations. You can only start with the current circumstances and choose ideal actions from here forward. Certainly, you can learn from the past, but you cannot change it, make poor decisions because of regret, or allow rancor to poison your team. Any part of a difficult situation that has been caused by unchangeable past actions or effects should be considered only in terms of remedies or consequences rather than attempting to apply retrospective wisdom.

- Your role is no longer only technical, so don't get hung up in what you think is technically correct or in supporting the stance you held as a technical contributor. Taking the side of someone you disagree with is a great way to show that you are supportive of your team, you are flexible in approach, and you are willing to compromise.

- If you can take meditated action to resolve a problem without severe adverse effects, then do it. This seems like a simple and obvious statement, but quick and easy action is often opposed by a mental block for new managers. The need to consult company policy or the need to spend precious time considering the issue, or even a lack of confidence in what is and is not your responsibility can all interfere with your ability to make good spontaneous decisions.

- Spend more time listening than talking. When you encounter a difficult situation, ask simple questions (even if you think you already know the answer) and listen carefully until you have exhausted all information sources.

- Accept ideas when you can, propose alternatives when you can't. If you must reject an idea, find out what result is being sought and get that same effect from a different action; otherwise explain why it is not possible.

- Take tangible actions as a result of listening and follow up with communication about what actions you and others have taken.

- Communicate accurately. Successful management is not about interpreting results in a favorable light or hiding risks. It's not about making people sacrifice themselves, and it's not about misrepresenting the truth. Tell the story straight to everyone. If it is confidential, tell them so, and explain why.

- Remember that everyone around you has less information than you do because you are the manager. Individual contributors know about their own efforts but not about all of the other efforts or the overall plan. Upper management knows about the goals and the costs but not about the individual risks and resources. Often, the source of difficulties is simply the lack of communication.

- Capture the passion of team members by intervening in stress or conflict situations, winning them some point that they desperately want, and at once getting them to make a choice that you need. Form a solid opinion of the skills and abilities of each specific person in every key area so you know what to expect. Everyone earns his or her place by productivity on the current project—no room for favors, cliques, or tiers.

PERFORMANCE FEEDBACK

Even if no other situations challenge you in your management role, you will always need to provide performance feedback. Your team members may all be doing a good job, and you should tell them so. But they will not improve and grow if you don't point out their weaknesses and performance gaps; they will not respect your positive perspective if it does not have a complementary category of "opportunities to improve."

The need for feedback is based on that—finding improvements. If you can make your team members more productive, that will be a positive result for you on your current project and a positive result for team members for the rest of their careers. As an emerging manager, you have the advantage of having very recently been in the role that your team members are performing. You know it and remember it well. You probably have a well-formed opinion of how team members could improve—a ready font of inspiration, if only you can get your message across.

CHAPTER 10 - DIFFICULT SITUATIONS

MIKE'S MANAGEMENT USE CASE

An expert developer was hired as a key contributor on a project with me at a start-up. There was not a clear leadership structure, but we were all highly competent professionals with enough experience to pull together. That plan was fine until the supposed expert started making obvious mistakes, and it became clear that supposed competencies were fabricated.

I escalated the problem, but there was little management bandwidth for my team so nothing was done. The "expert" started avoiding me and other team members as much as possible—oftentimes not even coming to work. Deadlines approached, and we went into overdrive to make up for the loss of a team member who, unfortunately, was still on the payroll.

When I finally got some management attention on the situation, I was told to start my evaluation of the expert all over by documenting clear goals and tracking progress in written communication, supervised by the manager, on a weekly basis. And I was told to be more tolerant of new employees because some of this situation must have also been my fault. I felt powerless, overworked, and cheated. I wanted out!

But then I realized I was thinking like a toddler who just says "it's unfair" when things don't go the right way. I took a step back and worked on

> understanding what happened as a formal prob-
> lem, with symptoms and a solution, including
> things like recycles and defects. I stayed with the
> company for ten more years; the alleged expert
> and the manager were gone within six months.

You may be tempted to keep your thoughts to yourself
and not provide any feedback to others, thus avoiding many difficult situations. But by doing that, you are
communicating falsely that you have no comment or
recommendation for improvement. By denying team
members the benefit of your guidance, you are limiting
their potential for growth. If you need additional motivation to summon the sincerity that you need to provide
direct feedback, consider the following two points:

- Everyone on the team recognizes poor performance
  and they will question your own competence if you
  do not do something about it.

- If you encounter a cost management situation that requires you to let go of a member of your team, chances
  are that you will remove the weakest one. Don't wait
  for that low moment to finally communicate sincerely.
  Or when you are dividing a fixed raise budget among
  a number of people, you have to be prepared to explain to each person what they got. Again, if the raise
  conversation is the first time someone hears from you
  sincerely, it will be a very difficult and unfair situation.

In the immediate, these discussions are uncomfortable to say the least. Yet most people will tell you that

they would prefer to hear the feedback, no matter how harsh it is, so that they have a chance to improve.

You may also be uncomfortable giving feedback to people who are older and more experienced than you. A unique aspect of a software development career is that rapid change in technology can erase a great deal of the value of many years of experience. So when you make a move into managing software developers, it is likely that even in your very first role, you will be supervising and directing people who are much older than you. In fact, the abilities that differentiate you from them may simply be that you have made the move into management, demonstrating leadership. All that really matters is that you understand your role, and they understand theirs—someone has to be in charge and that's you. It's not personal, and it should not be emotional; it's just a fact.

HONZA'S MANAGEMENT USE CASE

Once you move into management, you will often be exposed to all sorts of situations in which the established authority charts are reversed or redrawn. You will manage people who are older than yourself. You will manage people who clearly have more knowledge in certain areas than you. You will manage people who were previously your peers or even your bosses! Those situations will initially bring some discomfort and uneasiness, but you will likely be surprised at how quickly the new order of things falls into place.

Something you may recall from your experience prior to management is that there is a bond of camaraderie and often friendship among the people who are specifically *not* in management. As you begin to formulate opinions and communicate them, you will start creating a separation between yourself and others. A lesson to learn fast as an emerging manager is that your team members are not your friends. They may be friends outside of work, but on the job, they are your employees. If you are confused about this point, you may treat different people unfairly, fail to communicate with the right strength, or even overlook a problem you would have otherwise spotted.

Your feedback has to be honest, heartfelt, objective, and complete—unbiased and unbounded by distractions. Before entering any difficult situation, you need to ensure that your own perspective is grounded. Free yourself of your biases and opinions so that you can resolve the situation in the clearest way possible.

Different people take feedback in different ways. Some people will get motivated when they hear critique; some will be disappointed by it. But nearly universally,

- Everyone needs to hear it and will at least consider whether your opinion is valid even if they deny your direction.

- Everyone takes feedback better when they hear from you that they have done a good job on important work beforehand. A spoonful of sugar makes the medicine go down.

A NOTE ON POOR PERFORMERS

Poor performers in software development actually detract from the total output capability of a team. By asking the same questions repeatedly, breaking build processes, recycling too many times through the same defects, completing tasks late, and always being distressed, these individuals drag down the performance of the team. Others who are doing a good job will see their efforts put in jeopardy by poor performers. They will lose confidence in the company for recruiting and retaining team members who cannot hold their own, and they will lose confidence in the emerging manager for not dealing swiftly and definitively with the problem.

Your job is to formulate a direct and accurate message about the individual's performance and to communicate that message in a planned one-on-one meeting. In fact, doing so as often as necessary is a great way to make sure your team knows you are aware of what's happening and that you're not afraid to communicate feedback. Once they expect it from you, they will take feedback less personally and more professionally.

If you delay feedback, pile it up and "dump" it on people, you will cause fear and confusion. If you provide it consistently, quickly after specific events, you will most certainly condition better performance from the team. When you perform periodic required "appraisals" or "reviews," as required by standard personnel processes, recall these feedback sessions and incorporate what you've already communicated into the formal framework.

Make mistakes providing feedback rather than working on building the perfect message that gets delivered late or never. As long as you know there is a problem, raise it for discussion, so you will have a chance to talk through it. Base your initial feedback on facts and generalize a pattern if you think there is one. As the discussion progresses, cite specific examples and refine your own opinion about the problem. Just the fact that you held the discussion is already valuable as a part of the ongoing relationship you have with your team; if your feedback is accepted and results in improvement, then you've scored a win.

MIKE'S MANAGEMENT USE CASE

A legendarily prolific developer was on my team to deliver the first phase of a multiyear project. His reputation was spectacular, and I could tell it was all true. Within six weeks, we were in our first iteration cycle and the volume of his accomplishments was astounding.

The initial quality results for his work were solid as well. In code reviews, though, we had a big problem. His work was difficult to understand for anyone who came after him. The style problems were classic—few comments in the code, short variable names, very long functions, etc. I asked his previous manager about this, and the reply I got shocked me: "Why be so critical of such a talented person!"

One good reason, of course, would be to help that talented person become even more talented. Another good reason would be to make sure that the great work he did would be in service for a long, long time because it was simple to maintain.

Certainly this developer was proud and even arrogant, but he was actually glad to hear direct and clear criticism because he thought many other developers needed to work on their style too, and if he was getting read the riot act, others probably were also. He did not improve much, but at least I know I tried!

Once you get to know your team members, you will learn how they react to feedback. There are many different dimensions of these reactions, but some of the classics are:

- Comfort Zone people. Some people will not accept or act on your feedback because it would push them out of their comfort zone. You may have tried to influence their performance, but they won't improve unless you can be more explicit with them. Stronger critique may be needed to clarify the situation. You can determine when to use this method by first asking the individual to explain back to you what you have communicated. If they have understood you and they still don't want to take any corrective action, you should progressively become more direct.

- Perfectionists. Some people are not able to accept any criticism because it demoralizes them. Your relentless focus on helping them improve comes across as an ongoing accusation of failure. Be very fair and appeal to common sense. These individuals may try to talk you into retracting your critique, but you should avoid that unless new facts are introduced that you previously lacked. Otherwise, stick to your guidance.

HONZA'S MANAGEMENT USE CASE

Be prepared for perfectionists in such denial of any criticism that attempts to provide feedback may permanently damage your relationship with them and even cause them to flee your company. That is a very hard prospect to face, but withholding feedback is not a valid option in most environments.

Someone I once supervised was a smart, if junior, developer who had only been with the company for a short time. I gave him an evaluation that was generally positive, pointing out various accomplishments, but also including the usual section that featured opportunities for improvement. After we went through the document, he was completely crushed. He dismissed the positive feedback as self evident but dwelled on the negative points. He admitted that there was some truth to it, but argued that I had no right to bring it up because he was so exceptional and talented in other areas.

I stood my ground and patiently explained my position as he argued, begged, told stories from his past, and argued some more. In the end, we agreed to work on those areas and set some specific goals which would demonstrate improvement. But his attitude changed completely. He lost his confidence and drive, then slowly worked his way out of the company.

Always remember that people on the team are the ones who do the work. As a manager, you are there to make sure they have everything they need to be successful and to make sure that they are using those resources to the best of their ability to deliver. You serve them with passion and focus for success in every way that is needed. You show compassion for their troubles and difficulties, listening to their needs and being fair always.

Even when you are criticizing, because you are fair and informed, you are giving team members the ability to improve themselves. When you put capable people in a role of responsibility, value is created. You can improve the performance of your team through any means, be it training, by helping them see the need for improvements, or by assembling the right skills and personalities into a unit. Any way you do it, better team members deliver more value.

MIKE'S MANAGEMENT USE CASE

Every manager eventually faces an employee who threatens to leave the company "unless" demands are met. I've had employees bring in the newspaper "want ads" with jobs circled, showing higher pay. I've had employees float their resume on Internet job sites. I even experienced an information leak from a secure server that allowed everyone to know everyone else's salary, resulting in a particularly nasty rash of demands.

Certainly some of these confrontations are serious and based on a solid foundation that merits attention. But most of them are simply misguided or opportunistic, based more on emotion than on fact. In these cases, the employee is probably not really considering a job change.

While you should sincerely address each person one-on-one when they have concerns about compensation, it is possible to quickly determine who is serious and who is not. Consider your own decisions and frustrations—if you really thought that you might be changing companies, you would have several sources of reliable information about potential jobs. You would make a list of things that you wanted to achieve in your new role, covering things like opportunity, technology, and compensation. You would try to understand the investment you have already made in relationships and product knowledge at your current company, and the effort required to restart that process elsewhere. When you are talking to someone about compensation, probe these areas openly and make an assessment about whether they are educated enough to be considering a job change.

If you don't think they are serious, use the discussion as a time to highlight why you think they are valuable, why your company is the right one, and how you will help them grow. If you do think it's serious, engage human resources and your boss (but have a recommendation ready: a plan to retain and/or a reaction plan for their departure).

WHEN A PROJECT IS IN TROUBLE

Many difficult situations arise from the stresses of projects that begin to go off course. The term "turnaround manager" refers to experienced managers who are specifically adept at understanding and sorting out all of the problems in this sort of environment. But their skills are not needed in most common situations that you will encounter as a new manager. Instead, troubled projects are a great opportunity for you to produce real value for your company and build new skills for yourself by rapidly dealing with a series of difficult situations. Unlike one-on-one problems, the turnaround situation will not be confrontational. It will require you to muster strength and endurance from a team that seems to have none left. It will be uncomfortable for you, especially if you are not accustomed to leading people.

But it can also be fun. That's because in a turnaround, many of the rules of management appear to be suspended. Nothing about the plan is sacred if everyone believes the team is going to fail. As a developer, you may have accepted orders and continued blindly down a path even if you disagreed with what you were asked to do, simply because you thought you might not have enough information and, surely, someone making the decisions was competent. As a manager, it's your job to steward the resources in your care in order to deliver value to your business, at an increasing rate, regardless of the conditions before you took over, or after you move on. There's no point in working very hard as the manager just to make sure that when failure comes, you can say it's not your fault! Effort from some team members or from you is not important if the whole project fails because you all fail *together*. You have to turn the whole team around, not simply redouble your own efforts or focus on just some of the people.

WHEN IT'S TIME TO GET THE JOB DONE

Turning a project around starts with building your own conviction about what needs to happen. First, you have to get convinced that the project is important. Find out why the project exists (if you don't already know) in a way that you can explain clearly to others. Cut out any parts of the project (including deliverables) if there is no known justification for them. Teach your team about your customer's business if that is a way for them to understand the urgency of what needs to be done. Be patient with your team members individually but communicate urgency to them as a group.

246

Use commitment language rather than hedging. "We will" instead of "we might," or "you should" instead of "you can." A team that is in trouble first needs inspiration, especially if they are discouraged. You have to make your team members believe that it is possible to be successful, even if it requires the risk and sacrifices that you are going to ask them to take on. Your role as a manager is to project confidence about what is possible, not to doubt about what is unlikely. The fact is that there are many reasons why anything will fail, but the surest one is that the people working on it believe it will. The converse is just as true, and it's the manager's role to lead the team down a path that goes to success. The facts of risk and dangers should not be overlooked or hidden—they should be considered objectively and mitigated one by one.

A great management tool is to look for so called "low-hanging fruit." Seize opportunities to claim small victories that are immediately available. You may have to stretch at first—creating opportunities to celebrate simply because you need them. But a demoralized team (pretty much any team that is off track) will respond. Create milestones to fuel enthusiasm. Especially when you're new on a team, you need to show your team that you are a winner and that your leadership will carry them. Use that positive environment to explain that more effort is needed from everyone. Ensure that each person has a small goal to achieve in a faster-than-normal time line.

Next, look for a strategy that will make success *possible*. Your team members are logical, thinking beings, so they need a reason to believe that success is likely where previously it was not. This can be done by adjusting the scope or dates for the project, by getting more team members to help, or by bringing in incentives that will allow your team to justify the effort needed to succeed. Use simple concessions that are within your scope to boost motivation and show goodwill—equipment assignments, dinners, schedule flexibility, and so on. Keep the work productive and dynamic by spending a lot of your own time in the work area where your team operates.

MIKE'S MANAGEMENT USE CASE

Project plans can be complex or simple, depending on your own abilities and practices. A special version of a project plan that almost anyone can use for success is what I call a "home run plan." A home run applies to the last three or four weeks of any big effort, and it turns the project plan around so that time becomes the critical resource.

A home run plan can be expressed simply. Create a long list of everything that has to be done in the last days of a project, then put them all in the order in which they have to be done and attach specific dates to any of them that have a hardwired external date (code audit dates by third parties, test equipment schedule slots, etc.). Try to front-load the schedule so that most everything that can be done sooner is in the first week or two.

Now bring your team together and show them the plan. Let them add anything that is missing to the plan, but then toss out any preconceived notions about who is going to do which things. Instead, auction off all of the items, going point by point with assignments. Take a few assignments yourself. The idea is that when you're done with this, everyone knows how the team is going to pull off completing the project; things that are not so important are naturally set aside because everyone has something important to do—and, best of all, you have a daily plan to track against!

RECOVERY STRATEGIES

Every situation has its own recovery strategy, so you will have to create your own approach. But a number of techniques prove valuable in a pattern of turnaround experience:

- Face the customer yourself. Customers can be very stubborn about what is needed, and when, from your team. This can be an impossibly high barrier for a manager who struggles to manage external expectations *through other people*. Take the time to prepare a strong message with specifics of how the team will *fail* altogether under the current load (realistic, not emotional). You will find that customers are quickly willing to prioritize and break up functionality into multiple releases of smaller scope and longer time line if you can speak credibly about how you will deliver. This happens because most of the customers of software development teams are in the business world, where posturing and conviction are part and parcel of *negotiation*. If you clear the slate and convince them that you are not *negotiating,* but in fact you are *pleading* with them for their own good, they will agree.

- Change your development process. If your process forces you to serialize tasks, try to find a way to work them in parallel instead. Look for bulky efforts like formatting documentation or heavy testing that can be performed by unskilled temporary resources, or automated. If your dates are driven by one specific kind of client, tailor the efforts toward those needs instead of completing all requirements for all kinds of clients. Be careful not to destroy your project's future though! Seek permission to introduce these limitations even while you are taking action so you can ensure that the meta-damage is limited.

- Remove poor performers from the team. It is counter-intuitive to remove anyone from the team when the work is piling up and the deadline is approaching. But poor performers in software development actually drain productivity, causing more damage to the team than the small benefit they might add. Morale of other team members can be improved by removing poor performers as well—they will know that they are on a more exclusive team that merits extra effort.

- Money talks. This one is last for a reason—because it should be your last resort. Many people are not motivated by money, and oftentimes money causes more problems than it solves. But there are specific instances, such as when a key resource that is motivated by money can be given an incentive to work nights and weekends for a short stretch of time. Don't approach money as a motivator lightly and always seek advice from experienced managers before pursuing this option.

MIKE'S MANAGEMENT USE CASE

I once counseled a manager when he asked me about getting his team to work long hours toward a looming deadline. He said he had tried motivating people with soft things like bringing in dinners and showing late-night movies at the office. Everyone understood that the goals were urgent to the *company*, but they would not make even the slightest *personal* sacrifice for the sake of the deadline.

Together, we explored options like bonuses and communications—just asking people to work hard—and yet nothing made sense in the very short time that remained. So we decided to do an experiment. I asked him to get a stack of fresh $100 bills using the little bonus pool that he had available. Since "quitting time" was 5:00 p.m., I asked him to walk around at 5:15 handing out $100 to anyone who was still at the office. When asked why each person received the money, he was to hint at the idea that there would be similar actions on other days, but at later times. There was never a formal explanation of any organized bonus program. When news spread the next day, a few people stayed longer and it was well worth the expense.

CLOSURE

It's hard to face problems. But people expect leaders to take on tough jobs, and the spotlight is on you. Fortunately, a formula of objective consistency and open communications will help you solve most of the situations you encounter.

Performance problems with team members and projects that get in trouble are two common types of difficult situations. In these cases and others, don't delay action beyond the time that you need to make a good and informed decision. Afterward, with the benefit of hindsight, think constructively about what you might do differently under similar circumstances in the future. But avoid dwelling needlessly on what you might have done differently this time; what's done is done and you need to move on.

––––––––––

Chapter 11

BEYOND EMERGENCE: CAREERS IN MANAGEMENT

Above the line-level direct contributor, all companies are made up of people whose job is management. The role of a manager gets more abstract with increasing responsibility, and of course doing it well requires growing knowledge and expertise. But the goal of achieving results through other people does not change as a fundamental competency at any level. Higher up the hierarchy, the job becomes more and more removed from the actual work product of the specific company. Great managers learn at each level, stretching their ability to manage through others while remaining in touch with what is really happening, no matter how far removed. Easier said than done!

MIKE'S MANAGEMENT USE CASE

A big client took my company by surprise, and suddenly I found myself recruiting most of a new team while trying to get work started as quickly as possible. We found one new recruit, but we were still at least two people short going into a critical time for delivery.

Interviews and other recruiting activities compounded the schedule crunch and distracted everyone. I had to make a quick decision: stop recruiting and try to pull it off with the team at hand or keep up the recruiting and put the team further at risk of burnout. With buy in from the team, I was able to reach a compromise.

We did stop recruiting, but I got some of the money that was set aside for new recruits and put it in a bonus pool. Everyone worked very hard for too long, but they had a guaranteed payday and they were able to prepare their families for the sacrifice that was needed. We pulled it off, albeit without any long-term benefits for the team.

The popular media and our own experiences generally paint a poor picture of upper management. Why strive for a career in management when ultimately so few management careers yield "rock star" status (Welch, Iacocca), and so many result in scandals and apparent disappointment? What's worse, upper management is the butt of many jokes. Managing deeper and deeper organizations, it is easy to inadvertently slip out of touch with what most people at the company actually do. When most of your time is spent addressing abstract issues like profitability and expansion rather than people, customers and products, staying "in touch" can become a secondary priority. Once this occurs, a manager may feel a great deal of empowerment and potential, no longer encumbered by the details of the day-to-day, but in fact a decline toward management failure has already begun.

HOW THOSE "ROCK STARS" AVOID THE PROBLEM

There are great managers who don't fall prey to this trap. One common trait they all carry is a need to remain engaged, to some degree, with the difficult human side of their business. Why do customers buy the product? Why do employees choose to join the company? How are future managers trained, and what are the values instilled in them? Certainly all of these qualitative fields have to be balanced with ambition for profit growth. For the emerging manager, the solution is to design and implement an approach—Jack Welch calls it an operating system, and his is on a *much* larger scale—that turns the amorphous, organic complexity of management into a compartmentalized, digitized process. A system gives you a broad perspective about what is happening while still letting you tackle details every day.

Imagine a company as a complex machine consisting of active parts like motors and valves, which are controlled by successively higher knobs and levers. Very close to the action of the machine, the management controls are specific and direct regulators of devices. But groups of these management controls have to be regulated by indirect controls such as an overall throttle of output or a power management function. Still higher, the system is monitored for failures or performance problems. Next is a tier of controls that regulates production mode, maintenance mode, complete shutdown, etc. And above that, a decision process determines when to replace systems, when to do maintenance, and so forth.

Inside such a machine, the difference between the job of a valve and that of a gauge is clear. But, as a manager inside the machine, the job of sitting at the controls is apparently the same as you rise through the chain of control rooms. By having worked at the bottom and then in successively higher posts, the purpose and processes at every level will be clear to you. It is advantageous to have become proficient as a manager of smaller scope when you are given a bigger challenge.

The machine analogy can be used quite literally to understand your career in management:

- What does the machine do? Know the purpose of the product or service you are delivering. At every level in your management career, a relentless focus on the goal of the company will always guide you well—around others who have lost the right direction, toward improvements that are truly valuable, away from distractions.

- How does the machine work? Know the means by which your product or service achieves a valuable purpose and how your current role forms part of that broader whole. This will empower you to eliminate wasteful efforts within your scope that do not contribute toward your assigned purpose, to inspire people with a true vision for improvement. It will give you a map with which to guide your career. It will even provide insight into the company's future. Many new managers fail to understand this point.

They get stuck waiting for orders to come from above when they should be taking innovative actions unprompted.

- Which components are most important and how can you foretell trouble in one of these? Again, like a machine, large organizations depend on key parts. Ask yourself which of your own areas of responsibility (people, customers, and products) could derail your success and how you could prevent such a failure.

- Which path ahead is the right one for you? As your management career progresses, you work for a series of more and more powerful people. Each one has a broader vision, more powerful counterparts in other departments or divisions, and a more compelling allure to draw out followers. Part of the role of management is vision, but hollow vision that is not substantiated by results can be difficult to spot, especially when you are following a fast-climbing leader. Know how your products produce profits because of what they do for your customers; know how your customers choose products because of their needs. These beacons will separate the charlatans and powerbrokers from the true achievers that you should follow.

MIKE'S MANAGEMENT USE CASE

A new developer on my team was reporting to an inexperienced manager, and the two of them were not communicating well. The developer felt that the manager was taking credit for his work.

The manager felt that the developer was being abrasive and uncooperative.

This went on for over a month, and it was clear that one of the two of them would soon leave our company. I dug in and discussed the situation with each of them separately. I am confident that the problem was on both sides—I went back and forth relaying what they each said until finally I convinced them to speak to each other honestly.

I got the manager to be more humble and re-member that his role as manager was to support the developer. I got the developer to understand that managers need to get status updates and re-port on them to superiors because that's their job. They are both very successful people, each in his best role.

When you begin to manage team leads, it will be impor-tant for you to support them in their efforts to *lead*. For example, ensure that you provide them with important information to communicate with their team members. Let them communicate the information so that they are seen as empowered and "in the know." Your own com-munication with their team members should be more abstract and vision oriented, so they will look to their team leader for concrete, specific direction.

YOUR MISSION STATEMENT

Your management program is a detailed, ever-growing set of documents, practices and solutions that have worked for you in the past. The program allows you to do the management job consistently every day. But your management career will not stay within the confines of events you know how to handle. To guide you beyond those borders, you will need a broader, more visionary perspective. Write yourself a *mission statement*.

What do you most like to do and why is that going to make you better in a management capacity? Identify the key attributes that are needed to achieve your vision (you may need to discuss these with a mentor; it can be awkward at first to talk about yourself but it really helps!) and give yourself some time to work on them. Create a thematic approach that will help you identify with your job in management and will help your team understand what drives you:

- You may be in management because of a vision that you want to fulfill for the company, with benefits to its people through growth and profitability.

- Or you may be about the growth of people first, assuming the best people will build the best company.

- Another possibility is that you are about social values, with benefits to the world from the multiplied efforts of your labor for a higher purpose.

- Or among thousands of others, you may be "about" the technology and evolution of products, with all other benefits flowing from this font of business value.

Your mission is as distinct and creative as you are yourself. The best guidance for the mission statement is to make it something you believe you will still support in three years' time. That does not mean you can't change it over time, but it should not be something that is so time boxed that your team fails to see it as principle and instead treats it as a short-term goal.

SUCCESSFUL TEAMS

In your first leadership role, you will have little control over who is on your team and what task you are given. But if you achieve a few goals, those early efforts will quickly pay off and result in a broader scope of responsibility. When this happens, you will encounter a new challenge: setting up successful teams that you will manage through a *team lead*. This happens naturally as your ability and scope increase. Just how you set up the team and whom you place in the leadership role will make or break your success. Your management program cannot neglect this area—it is very important to get it right, and there are many ways in which you will be led to the *wrong* approach.

It is natural for your superiors, for example, to use their limited knowledge of which people you have available and suggest how you should organize. Individuals on your team will pick favorite coworkers and demand choice assignments. You will be expected to work with the people you have been given, regardless of their skills. Finally, everyone will assume that a team that has been working together for some time (usually regardless of how well) will stay that way.

It is as if your role as manager were not needed and everyone would be just fine *without* you. Except for one little thing: nobody wants to be *responsible* for results because that part is still your job! Make no mistake, the team assignments are your decision and no one else's. You need all the inputs you can get, but you absolutely cannot afford to expect spontaneous self-organization. Your role in this process should be very active—have many discussions, often to the point of wearing down your patience. Compromise where you can, but give yourself some principles and stick to them.

PRINCIPLES OF SUCCESSFUL TEAMS

The goal is to make the whole of the team achieve more than the sum of its parts. How will you find the strengths of each person? How will you choose to use the strengths of each in order to build out a whole working team? Motivating each person is a different challenge altogether—once you know what you want from them, your job is to create the environment where it can happen.

Here are some of the principles that could be used to guide the team creation process. Clearly you are con-strained by the people and other resources available to you, but be sure to consider and propose trades with other managers where appropriate—don't assume anything is off-limits. Once you know what you have on hand, you are ready to make a plan.

BALANCED DIMENSIONS

Your teams should approach a balance of personality and capability attributes that will get meta-results of *growth for people* and a *broad perspective for your product*. Think about each person in the context of the project, and ask yourself what they are going to gain in the process of making the team more successful. Examples:

- Experience level: by mixing experienced and inexperienced people, you will refresh each of them with the other's capabilities naturally, without the forced confines of a training seminar or management coaching.

- Passion: people who are passionate about *quality* should be balanced with those who are passionate about *delivery*. Neither is useful without the other, and they will learn this when they deliver more value as a team.

- Attitude: lighthearted people can bring levity to tense situations; intensely focused people can ensure that the levity does not get out of control. They will each benefit from exposure to the other.

APPROPRIATE SKILLS AND CAPACITY

Match skills on the team to the projects at hand. Ensure that you are providing growth for some people, but don't count on too much capacity from a person who is making a big change in his or her technology skill set. Similarly, balance resources between teams according to the size of the effort that is needed. All projects are not created equal.

EXPERTISE AND PRODUCTIVITY

People on your team are not created equal either. You know who the stars are, who the rising stars are, and who is clearly not in either category. Give every team someone who is going to help ensure success by being the technical expert. Make sure that every rising star has a clear mentor on his or her team to help them pull ahead.

NOTHING TO SPARE

When your teams are ready, don't force everyone you have left into a project. Instead, propose that these team members could move on to other projects on other teams with a different manager. Be careful, but don't be afraid to take this step—it will give you a high degree of respect because the instinct of "political" managers is to hoard people rather than to operate efficiently.

CO-LOCATION

As a principle, it is important for teams to be located together at work. This is a traditional view, and it is certainly challenged by the globalization of software development. Still, in-person interaction is undeniably important. If you do have teams that are spread far apart, do everything in your power to use technology as a unifier. Webinars, teleconferences, and the like can provide a great environment for team meetings and other aspects of management once you get used to the quirks of remote management.

TEAM LEADS

When your scope grows large, say above ten or twelve people, you *must* delegate management of distinct teams to a team lead. Fight the instinct to manage multiple projects yourself. You may have a high tolerance for multitasking, and most people may prefer for you to be their team lead, but think about the future and choose team leads that you will manage:

- It is possible for you to box yourself into the role of leading a team just as you might have when you were in a technical individual contributor role. Placing leads in charge of teams is a way of proving that you are ready to manage a larger scope.

- Emerging managers on your teams need a path that you can provide to help them emerge. Remember meta-results and think of the value you are creating by letting future managers come forward in a nurturing environment. There must be growth in an organization, or the best people will leave.

- If you get a reputation as a manager who helps high-potential people find good career paths, you will find that these people will seek you out and choose to be on your team. That's fuel for your own career and theirs!

- When you are away, such as for vacations or participating in responsibilities related to your growing management scope, it is important to have clear second-in-command people who will make progress without you. Among these, you will find a successor who will make it possible for you to accept your next big role.

WORK/LIFE BALANCE

As you get more and more responsibility and have to handle more projects or larger teams, you will inevitably face the question of how to keep up to speed with all your personal and professional obligations. Working harder or longer may help for a while, but it will allow you to scale yourself only so much. A day has only 24 hours and even Edison had to sleep four of those.

Don't fall for the trap of working hard just to show everyone else how inadequate they are, or how indispensible you have become. As the number of hours you put in each week grows, the quality of your work and of your decisions will necessarily decline. That is a terrible prospect if you are accountable for the work of many people!

The key to success is to work smarter, not just harder. Obviously, that is easier said than done, but you should already be equipped with some necessary skills after reading this book:

- Delegate what you can.

- Do not put yourself into the critical path for any project.

- If you still have too much work, delegate some more.

- Finally, if you delegated all that you could and you still have more than you can accomplish with balance and quality in any given day, the solution is to **prioritize**. Not everything needs to be done immediately. You are not required in every possible meeting. Not all actions have the same impact and importance, so treat them that way. Set expectations with the people who will be affected, and simply leave some tasks for later… or remove them from your "to do" list altogether.

You may get challenged on some of the tasks and you may need to adjust your priorities; that is normal and you should expect it. Apply your best judgment and understanding of the state of the business each day. Pick the things that are most important and try to *complete* them. *Getting stuff done* is far more important than *working on stuff*.

If you are in this job for the long haul, you need to find a work pattern that will allow you to go on for years without burning out. Progression of your management career requires that you demonstrate the ability to handle a growing load without getting buried by it. Family life and hobbies should remain a priority for your health and mental fitness.

Some people find it useful to set ground rules that they do not question, such as "I never work on Saturday when I go surfing" or "I never work between 6 and 9 PM when I am spending time with my family". There will be moments when you will have to violate these rules, but most of the time they should allow you to have time for yourself without feeling guilty that you are not working. As long as you put maximum effort into your job during work hours, you should be able to spend quality time while you are away.

CLOSING TOPICS

We've captured a few short topics here that should provide some input for you in the growth of your management career:

Never *crave* a formal title. This is a hang-up of many ambitious people, including those who move into management from technical ranks. The bottom line is that titles are not the substance of what you do, and they rarely reflect your true level of responsibility. Do the job first; ask for the title last. Promotions are easy when they are obvious. When unclear, they are tough. You can "fight" for a promotion and title, only to find that nothing changes because, after all, it's a paper exercise. Reserve your struggles for things that are worthwhile, like choice assignments, compensation increases, specific team members that you need, and growth opportunities.

Go "above and beyond" to support and *own* projects that your team has *completed*. This is not to say that you should personally get buried in details of defects and field reports from deployed software packages, or to take ownership away from other teams after you have moved on. But if you are proud of what your team has done and no one has provided for a maintenance path to make it successful, then you should be willing to work with your team to find a way to keep ownership, even after moving on to new projects and goals. Obviously, this should be discussed with your management and considered carefully. The alternative may be that someone else undoes the great things you have created! You will find that this "long shadow" of old projects is a great way to build meta-results for your team members as they learn to balance client priorities with the elegance of new designs.

No matter what level you achieve in management, always enjoy the products of your company. Know the features and concepts, the most important uses and the value proposition for clients. You will find people ready and willing to provide demonstrations and quite understanding of your ignorance when you ask even the most basic questions. Your attention is an opportunity for people to show off and feel important—a meta-result that will pay off in productivity and creativity, providing a big multiplier for the short time you invest.

MIKE'S MANAGEMENT USE CASE

A leadership team is a group of managers over different areas who meet as peers to plan department or business unit activities. Being part of a leadership team is a very powerful formative experience that you should embrace enthusiastically.

At first, you may feel that you have nothing in common with the other managers because their scope may span activities like technical publications, remote support, or sales. But what you will quickly find out is that their key issues are intimately connected to yours, their personnel problems are identical to yours, and their passion for success will inspire you.

I was fortunate to be part of such a team during a critical phase of a young operating unit. Meetings began every Tuesday at 7:00 a.m. and ran until 9:00 a.m., with eleven overly caffeinated people packed in to an eight-person room. In that pressure cooker, the VP who was in charge let us decide how to run the business. We always started with an agenda of must-discuss items but many other topics were introduced ad hoc. I gained a great deal of respect for every one of my peers, and for the company and VP who had assembled us.

Keep the concept of a leadership team alive in all of your management roles. Make a leadership team within your own group once you have a scope of responsibility that is large enough to demand it. Bring together the leaders who report to you, state the challenges that you want to resolve, and step back while they sort it all out. You can even invite one or two people you are considering for leadership roles. Of course you have to lead the discussion with questions and document the conclusions just as you did when you were coaching technical people on technical work.

More often than not, you will find that these meetings will make you and the leaders on your team more aware and more prepared for the next challenge of a career in management.

REFERENCES AND SUGGESTED READING

Brooks, F. P. 1978. *The Mythical Man-Month: Essays on Software Engineering*. New York: Addison-Wesley Longman Publishing.

Cantor, Murray. 2001. *Software Leadership: A Guide to Successful Software Development*. New York: Addison-Wesley Publishing.

Chan, Kim W., and R. Mauborgne. 2005. *Blue Ocean Strategy*. Boston: Harvard Business School Press.

Collins, J. 2001. *Good To Great*. New York: HarperCollins Publishers.

Deken, J. 1982. *The Electronic Cottage*. New York: William Morrow and Co.

Hunt, J. M., and J. R. Weintraub. 2002. *The Coaching Manager*. Thousand Oaks, California: Sage Publications.

Peters, T., and R. H. Waterman. 1988. *In Search Of Excellence*. New York: Grand Central Publishing.

Tracy, John A. 2004. *How to Read a Financial Report, 6th ed.* Hoboken, NJ: John Wiley and Sons.

Welch, J., and J. A. Byrne. 2001. *Straight From the Gut*. New York: Business Plus.

Whitehead, Richard. 2001. *Leading a Software Development Team: A Developer's Guide to Successfully Leading People and Projects*. New York: Addison-Wesley Publishing.